DATE DUE

JY 27 96			
JN 3 93			
AG 30 91			

Modern Critical Interpretations

William Shakespeare's
Julius Caesar

Modern Critical Interpretations

The Oresteia
Beowulf
The General Prologue to
  The Canterbury Tales
The Pardoner's Tale
The Knight's Tale
The Divine Comedy
Exodus
Genesis
The Gospels
The Iliad
The Book of Job
Volpone
Doctor Faustus
The Revelation of St.
  John the Divine
The Song of Songs
Oedipus Rex
The Aeneid
The Duchess of Malfi
Antony and Cleopatra
As You Like It
Coriolanus
Hamlet
Henry IV, Part I
Henry IV, Part II
Henry V
Julius Caesar
King Lear
Macbeth
Measure for Measure
The Merchant of Venice
A Midsummer Night's
  Dream
Much Ado About
  Nothing
Othello
Richard II
Richard III
The Sonnets
Taming of the Shrew
The Tempest
Twelfth Night
The Winter's Tale
Emma
Mansfield Park
Pride and Prejudice
The Life of Samuel
  Johnson
Moll Flanders
Robinson Crusoe
Tom Jones
The Beggar's Opera
Gray's Elegy
Paradise Lost
The Rape of the Lock
Tristram Shandy
Gulliver's Travels

Evelina
The Marriage of Heaven
  and Hell
Songs of Innocence and
  Experience
Jane Eyre
Wuthering Heights
Don Juan
The Rime of the Ancient
  Mariner
Bleak House
David Copperfield
Hard Times
A Tale of Two Cities
Middlemarch
The Mill on the Floss
Jude the Obscure
The Mayor of
  Casterbridge
The Return of the Native
Tess of the D'Urbervilles
The Odes of Keats
Frankenstein
Vanity Fair
Barchester Towers
The Prelude
The Red Badge of
  Courage
The Scarlet Letter
The Ambassadors
Daisy Miller, The Turn
  of the Screw, and
  Other Tales
The Portrait of a Lady
Billy Budd, Benito Cer-
  eno, Bartleby the Scriv-
  ener, and Other Tales
Moby-Dick
The Tales of Poe
Walden
Adventures of
  Huckleberry Finn
The Life of Frederick
  Douglass
Heart of Darkness
Lord Jim
Nostromo
A Passage to India
Dubliners
A Portrait of the Artist as
  a Young Man
Ulysses
Kim
The Rainbow
Sons and Lovers
. Women in Love
1984
Major Barbara

Man and Superman
Pygmalion
St. Joan
The Playboy of the
  Western World
The Importance of Being
  Earnest
Mrs. Dalloway
To the Lighthouse
My Antonia
An American Tragedy
Murder in the Cathedral
The Waste Land
Absalom, Absalom!
Light in August
Sanctuary
The Sound and the Fury
The Great Gatsby
A Farewell to Arms
The Sun Also Rises
Arrowsmith
Lolita
The Iceman Cometh
Long Day's Journey Into
  Night
The Grapes of Wrath
Miss Lonelyhearts
The Glass Menagerie
A Streetcar Named
  Desire
Their Eyes Were
  Watching God
Native Son
Waiting for Godot
Herzog
All My Sons
Death of a Salesman
Gravity's Rainbow
All the King's Men
The Left Hand of
  Darkness
The Brothers Karamazov
Crime and Punishment
Madame Bovary
The Interpretation of
  Dreams
The Castle
The Metamorphosis
The Trial
Man's Fate
The Magic Mountain
Montaigne's Essays
Remembrance of Things
  Past
The Red and the Black
Anna Karenina
War and Peace

These and other titles in preparation

William Shakespeare's
Julius Caesar

Edited and with an introduction by
Harold Bloom
Sterling Professor of the Humanities
Yale University

Chelsea House Publishers ◇ *1988*
NEW YORK ◇ NEW HAVEN ◇ PHILADELPHIA

© 1988 by Chelsea House Publishers, a division
of Chelsea House Educational Communications, Inc.,
    345 Whitney Avenue, New Haven, CT 06511
    95 Madison Avenue, New York, NY 10016
    5068B West Chester Pike, Edgemont, PA 19028

Introduction © 1988 by Harold Bloom

Printed and bound in the United States of America

10 9 8 7 6 5 4 3 2 1

∞The paper used in this publication meets the minimum requirements of the American National Standard for Permanence of
Paper for Printed Library Materials, Z39.48-1984

Library of Congress Cataloging-in-Publication Data
William Shakespeare's Julius Caesar / edited and with an
introduction by Harold Bloom.
        p.   cm. — (Modern critical interpretations)
    Bibliography: p.
    Includes index.
    Summary: A collection of nine critical essays on the Shakespeare
tragedy, arranged in chronological order of their original
publication.
    ISBN 0–87754–928–1 : $19.95
    1. Shakespeare, William, 1564–1616. Julius Caesar.   2. Caesar,
Julius, in fiction, drama, poetry, etc. [1. Shakespeare,
William, 1564–1616. Julius Caesar.   2. Caesar, Julius, in fiction,
drama, poetry, etc.   3. English literature—History and criticism.]
    I. Bloom, Harold, II. Series.
    PR2808.W54 1988
    822.3'3 — dc 19

ontents

Editor's Note / vii

Introduction / 1
    HAROLD BLOOM

Julius Caesar: The Roman Tragedy / 5
    DEREK TRAVERSI

Ritual and *Julius Caesar* / 29
    LAWRENCE DANSON

Dream and Interpretation: *Julius Caesar* / 43
    MARJORIE B. GARBER

Julius Caesar: Social Order
and the Kinetic World / 53
    MICHAEL LONG

"Thou Bleeding Piece of Earth": The Ritual Ground
of *Julius Caesar* / 61
    NAOMI CONN LIEBLER

Rhetoric in Ancient Rome / 79
    ANNE BARTON

The Roman Actor: *Julius Caesar* / 91
    JONATHAN GOLDBERG

Brutus's Nature and Shakespeare's Art / 105
    A. D. NUTTALL

Ironic Heroism in *Julius Caesar:* A Repudiation
of the Past / 121
    JAMES C. BULMAN

Chronology / 133

Contributors / 135

Bibliography / 137

Acknowledgments / 139

Index / 141

Editor's Note

This book brings together a representative selection of the best modern critical interpretations of William Shakespeare's *The Tragedy of Julius Caesar.* The critical essays are reprinted here in the chronological order of their original publication. I am grateful to Edward Jefferson for his assistance in editing this volume.

My introduction speculates upon the limits of Brutus as tragic hero and the relation of those limits to Shakespeare's own rather uncharacteristic, nearly stoic restraint in composing *Julius Caesar.* Derek Traversi commences the chronological sequence of criticism by considering the play as a contrast between the personal integrity of Brutus and the way of a Roman world that increasingly exiles such integrity.

In Lawrence Danson's reading, the sacrifice of Brutus serves the ritualistic ends of the tragedy, a view consonant with Marjorie B. Garber's analysis of the role of dream in the play, which she finds concerning itself "with the strange blindness of the rational mind" to the irrational forces that control life.

Michael Long, invoking the visions of Schopenhauer and Nietzsche, locates the tragic flaws of Brutus as centering in his inadequate stance towards the polarities of a kinetic world. Ritual is again the concern in Naomi Conn Liebler's essay, which centers upon the Feast of the Lupercal and its function in the play. Another aspect of ancient Rome, its oratory rhetoric, is examined in relation to *Julius Caesar* by Anne Barton. Still another, the Roman theatre, is clarified as to its function in Shakespeare's Roman tragedy by Jonathan Goldberg.

A. D. Nuttall traces some of the complexities of Shakespeare's mimetic art in the representation of Brutus, after which James C.

Bulman concludes this volume with an exegesis of Shakespeare's freedom in using dramatic conventions with considerable irony in his version of the death of Caesar.

Introduction

The Tragedy of Julius Caesar is a very satisfying play, as a play, and
is universally regarded as a work of considerable aesthetic dignity.
We tend to read it first when we are in school, because it is so clear
and simple a drama that our teachers find it suitable for us there. I
have seen it only once on stage, once on television, and once as a
film, and found none of these three presentations quite adequate, the
problem in each case being with the actor who misplayed Brutus.
Directors and actors seem to place more of Hamlet in Brutus than
Shakespeare himself set there, and Brutus just cannot sustain Hamlet's aura. Hamlet scarcely can speak without extending our consciousness into the farthest ranges, but there is a narcissistic, rather
spoiled quality to the perhaps excessively noble Brutus, and he does
not achieve ghostlier demarcations, keener sounds, until his fortunes
begin to fail.

Modern critics find somewhat problematical Shakespeare's supposed political stance in *Julius Caesar*. Presumably Shakespeare, as
an Elizabethan royalist, is unhappy about the assassination of Caesar,
and yet Brutus is the tragic hero. Caesar is in decay, a touch vain-
glorious, the conqueror dwindled into a ruler who accepts flattery.
But however the politics of *Julius Caesar* are to be resolved, the play
seems problematical in no other respect. Its characters, including
even Brutus, are not endless to meditation, and its rhetoric does not
reverberate so as to suggest a beyond. There is no Marlovian element
in *Julius Caesar*, no hero-villains of Hermetic ambition or Machiavellian intensity, no surpassingly eloquent and outrageous overreach-
ers. Whether from North's Plutarch or from Seneca, or more likely
from a strain in his own nature, Shakespeare brings forth a Stoic
music with its own dying falls, but without a grudge or bias against
our given condition. Brutus essentially is a Stoic, acutely self-

1

conscious and self-regarding, with a touch of Virgil's Aeneas in him. But he has been too much admired in Rome, and he greatly admires himself. A. D. Nuttall is useful in contrasting Brutus and his Stoicism to Antony's affective opportunism:

> Brutus, the aristocrat, his theoretic Stoicism borne on a foundation of shame-culture, on ancient heroic dignity, belongs to the Roman past. He can do the Stoic trick (rather like "isolating" a muscle) of separating his reason from his passions but he cannot exploit his own motivating passions with the coolness of an Antony. With all his fondness for statuesque postures Brutus remains morally more spontaneous than Antony.

Where is Cassius on this scale of moral spontaneity? He plays upon Brutus in order to bring him into the conspiracy, but then yields to Brutus both as to Antony's survival and on granting Antony permission to speak at Caesar's funeral. When he yields a third time and consents, against his will, to stake everything upon battle at Philippi, he completes the irony of his own undoing and Caesar's ghost is avenged. The irony could be interpreted as a dialectic of conscience and affection, since Cassius politically seduced Brutus by exploiting the Stoic hero's moral spontaneity. Cassius is destroyed by Brutus's incompetent political and military decisions, to which Cassius yields out of affection, but also because he must accept the moral consequences of having seduced Brutus into leadership, the only role possible for Brutus in any enterprise.

Cassius is the one figure in the play who might have benefited by a touch of Marlovian force or antithetical intensity, but Shakespeare preferred to maintain his own Stoic control in representing a Stoic tragedy. We ought to marvel that Shakespeare, a year or so later, could venture upon the infinite by writing *Hamlet*, where every current is antithetical and far beyond merely rational controls. *Julius Caesar* has more in common with *Henry V* than with *Hamlet*, just as the two parts of *Henry IV* reach out to *As You Like It* and *Hamlet*. What is excluded from *Julius Caesar* is the madness of great wit, the exuberance of Falstaff, of Rosalind, and of one of the endless aspects of Hamlet. As we miss Falstaff in *Henry V*, so we miss someone, anyone, who could cause *Julius Caesar* to flare up for us. Shakespeare, with a curiously Stoic forbearance, subdued himself to his subject, though we do not know why.

The results of this uncharacteristic *ascesis* are surely mixed. We receive clarity and nobility, and lose nearly everything that makes Shakespeare unique. Dr. Samuel Johnson's summary speaks to this better than I can:

> Of this tragedy many particular passages deserve regard, and the contention and reconcilement of Brutus and Cassius is universally celebrated; but I have never been strongly agitated in perusing it, and think it somewhat cold and unaffecting, comparing with some other of Shakespeare's plays; his adherence to the real story, and to Roman manners, seems to have impeded the natural vigour of his genius.

Whatever the impediments, *Julius Caesar* is an anomaly among Shakespeare's mature plays in that it possesses his originality in language, to a fair degree, yet is almost wholly devoid of his principal originality in representation. Not even Brutus changes by listening to himself ruminate. How much difference can we hear between Brutus at the beginning of act 2 and Brutus near to the end of act 5? Brooding upon the probable change in a crowned Caesar, Brutus takes the responsibility of prophesying the change:

> It is the bright day that brings forth the adder,
> And that craves wary walking.

Poor Brutus, once embarked upon his venture, never encounters his own bright day. Shakespeare subtly allows the Stoic hero a continuous nobility down to the end, while also allowing Brutus to be deaf to the irony of his final self-praise:

> Countrymen,
> My heart doth joy that yet in all my life
> I found no man but he was true to me.

We wince, however sympathetic we find Brutus, since he seems to have forgotten Caesar's last words, with their shock that Brutus, of all men, should have been untrue to his friend Caesar. Brutus's "As Caesar lov'd me, I weep for him" does not linger in us, but we do remember Antony's bitter eloquence:

> For Brutus, as you know, was Caesar's angel.

Perhaps Shakespeare's politics did inhibit his profoundest powers in *Julius Caesar*. The tragedy of Brutus and the crime against the monarch could not be reconciled with one another, and Shakespeare, divided against himself, found he could not be wholly true to Brutus.

Julius Caesar: The Roman Tragedy

Derek Traversi

Shakespeare's major plays on Roman history span between them the supremely creative years of his dramatic career. The earliest of the three, *Julius Caesar*, was separated by no great distance in time from the two parts of *Henry IV* and *Henry V* and is concentrated, like these plays, upon the interplay of personal motives and public necessity; whilst the other two—*Antony and Cleopatra* and *Coriolanus*—belong to the dramatist's last years and combine an acute understanding of historical processes with the illuminating presence of a distinctive tragic vision. Thus variously situated in time, the plays, by bringing together into a mutually enriching unit two of the principal themes of Shakespeare's mature work—those expressed respectively in the historical chronicles and in the series of great tragedies which followed them—constitute one of the undoubted peaks of his achievement.

The historical matter of all three plays is principally derived from Plutarch's *Lives of the Noble Grecians and Romans,* as translated into English from the French of Amyot by Thomas North. The fact is important for an understanding of the plays themselves; for, whereas it is, generally speaking, true that Shakespeare's acknowledged masterpieces—*Hamlet, Macbeth, King Lear*—owe little more than the barest outline of their plots to the comparatively artless narratives from which they derive, in the Roman tragedies we are

From *An Approach to Shakespeare 2:* Troilus and Cressida *to* The Tempest. © 1969 by Derek Traversi. Hollis & Carter, 1969.

conscious of dealing with what might almost be called a collaboration. It is well known that long passages from North's highly workmanlike translation were almost directly versified by Shakespeare; but a comparison of the relevant passages shows that the dramatist, in following his original closely, was in fact developing his own conception, being fully himself. The style of these plays, far from reflecting a pedestrian process of versification, shows a unique combination of narrative lucidity, achieved through the easy, almost conversational use of spoken rhythms and vernacular phrases, with poetic intensities that flow effortlessly from this foundation whenever the state of the action so requires. By the side of these works, even some of the effects of the great tragedies seem to have been reached with effort, to represent a sensibility strained to the utmost in the intensity of its reaction to emotional stresses; whilst the verse of the final comedies seems at times to achieve its symbolic effects through conventions of greater and more artificial complexity.

The action of *Julius Caesar* turns, in the tense simplicity of its narrative, upon an event of unique historical importance. Round this event with its varied and often contrasted significances for the Elizabethan mind, Shakespeare has developed a pattern of political passions which answers to a closely knit dramatic plan. The early scenes show Caesar and his enemies converging upon the striking of a blow which has in its inevitability, in the universal concern it focuses upon itself, the quality of a tragic sacrifice. The deed itself and the action which follows from it lead, in the central episodes, to the conflict of public and personal motives involved in the clash of Brutus and Antony over the dictator's dead body. Finally, in the concluding stages, the consequences of the murder are revealed through their effect upon each of the contending parties. The conspirators, brought to see their motives in the unflattering light of reality, collapse into mutual recrimination and confessed futility; whilst, against a background of practical assertion and ruthless calculation of the odds, a new Roman order replaces that which has been destroyed.

In one sense, and in one sense only, the entire action is centred upon the murdered dictator. He disappears, it is true, at the end of the first half of the play, and his appearances before his elimination have been strangely brief and enigmatic; but the fact remains that, alive, the action turns upon him, and when he is dead his spirit remains, as Brutus unwillingly confesses, persistently and implacably alive. The emphasis, however, in the presentation of the character lies elsewhere, in a notable sense of discrepancy between the figure which the dictator, obliged by the force of circumstance, presents to the world and the reality of what he in fact is. From the first, his use of the impersonal royal style implies an effort to live self-consciously up to the requirements which his isolated and uneasy eminence imposes. "Always," in his own phrase (1.2.211), "I am Caesar," and in that "always" there is a sense of danger, of living poised over a void, an imminent disaster, which, as we approach him more closely, his behaviour repeatedly confirms. It is true that many of the initial intimations of weakness in Caesar—Cassius's ascription to him of physical feebleness, Casca's belittling report of his "swooning" in the market place (1.2.249)—come from his enemies, and are to be understood as the product of envy: but true also that these same incidents contribute to the impression of one whom his circumstances oblige to play out a role, a course moreover in which he is largely supported by a vanity which will at last contribute to his disaster.

The scene (2.2) in which Caesar is persuaded, against his intimate will, to go to the Capitol is in this respect revealing. As Calpurnia, shaken by premonitions which the elements confirm, presses him to stay at home he clings obstinately to the determination which his situation has imposed upon him. "Caesar shall go forth": the dangers that threaten him are always *behind* him, out of sight, waiting to assert themselves against a man whose position obliges him to outface them:

> when they shall see
> The face of Caesar, they are vanished.
>
> (2.2.11)

Upon this illusion of constancy the dictator's position, and with it the fortunes of the Roman world, depend.

Faced, indeed, by portents "beyond all use," threats to human conceptions of order and purpose, Caesar responds with what is at once the striking of an attitude and a touch of sincerity:

> What can be avoided
> Whose end is purposed by the mighty gods?
>
> (2.2.26)

In the light of this implicit fatalism the renewed affirmation which follows—"Caesar shall go forth"—must seem strangely obstinate. It is followed by a further insistence upon the pose which we have come to associate with his dignity, a stressing of self-consciousness which ends by insinuating the presence of the weakness it seeks to deny:

> Of all the wonders that I yet have heard,
> It seems to me most strange that men should fear;
> Seeing that death, a necessary end,
> Will come when it will come.
>
> (2.2.34)

The lines answer to that sense of fatality, of subjection to the temporal process, which is present as a factor limiting human choices in all Shakespeare's plays of this period. Against this pervasive influence, Caesar is engaged in building up an impression of consistency which began no doubt as a real reflection of greatness, but which his situation, and the destiny which covers all human actions, now imposes upon him.

Caesar is revealed, in fact, less as brave and consistent at this moment than as talking himself into consistency. Beneath this determination, however, weakness once more asserts itself. Calpurnia persuades him to a course which his own instincts have already insinuated; he acquiesces ("Mark Antony shall say I am not well"), even while clinging to the excuse that it is the frailty of others that has imposed this change of plan: "for thy humour I will stay at home." The arrival of Decius Brutus to escort him to the Senate brings to the surface the contradictions by which he is torn. Decius is to tell the senators that he "will not come to-day"; since it is false that he cannot, and that he "dare not," falser, only the bare affirmation of his will can meet the case:

> The cause is in my will: I will not come;
> That is enough to satisfy the senate.
>
> (2.2.71)

The retort reveals the arbitrary nature of the consistency which circumstance imposes upon Caesar. It also covers an inner uncertainty; the pose has taken possession of the man, and will from now on lead him to his fate.

After Caesar's account of Calpurnia's dream and Decius's in-genious exercise in interpretation—both expressed in the heightened, almost hysterical language which surrounds conspiracy through-out—Decius drives home his point by a highly effective combination of flattery with an appeal to the dictator's unavowed love of power. The Senate have decided to confer a crown upon "mighty Caesar," and if he does not attend the session, "their minds may change." More dangerously still, Decius emphasizes the mockery which may follow if the truth were known:

> It were a mock
> Apt to be rendered, for some one to say
> "Break up the senate till another time,
> When Caesar's wife shall meet with better dreams."
>
> (2.2.96)

The appeal to vanity supports that to ambition, and indifference to Calpurnia—reflected in an attitude towards her that surely stands in significant contrast to Brutus's tender treatment of Portia (2.1)—is present in both. Above all—and here Decius is careful to cover his daring with a profession of love—it will be whispered that the master of Rome is "afraid": a hint than which none is better calculated to play upon the strange complex of conflicting emotions at the dic-tator's heart.

With this last speech, Decius achieves his aim. The victim brushes aside all misgivings—"How foolish do your fears seem now, Calpurnia"—jokes with his enemies, and greets Antony with a manly jest. Throughout we feel a recovery of confidence, a readiness to accept willingly what has now become his fate. The emphasis on "friendship," on taking wine together, underlines the monstrous treachery afoot; only Brutus, standing aside from the main stream, "yearns" to think that appearances are "false," that "every like is not the same." From this moment, Caesar's history marches together with that of his enemies to converge at the base of Pompey's effigy.

Caesar, however, though he dominates the action by virtue of his public position, is in no sense the principal moving force of the tragedy. This is provided, in the early scenes, by Brutus, who, in seeking the clarification of his own motives, gives the action its dynamic quality. His initial reflections are already charged with im-plications of character:

> Vexed I am
> Of late with passions of some difference,
> Conceptions only proper to myself,
> Which give some soil perhaps to my behaviours.
>
> (1.2.39)

The expression, notably reminiscent of certain utterances of Hamlet, stresses the nature, essentially inward-looking and exploratory, of his dilemma. To this Stoic theorist, tied to the contemplation of his own virtue, the "passions" present themselves as disturbing elements, shadowing the unity and self-control which he craves as the key to action. It is of the nature of his conflict to be without communication, "proper" to himself alone; and this inwardness, the product of his character and of his assumptions about life, affects him, when uneasily stirred to action, as a blot upon the harmonious personality at which he aims, a "soil" upon the fair outward presentation of himself which he so persistently craves.

It is the function of Cassius, by playing upon this desire for communication, to mould him to ends not finally his own. The peculiar relationship between the pair, and the method of its dramatic presentation, are both indicated in the query which opens his attack and in Brutus's reply:

> CASSIUS: Tell me, good Brutus, can you see your face?
> BRUTUS: No, Cassius: for the eye sees not itself
> But by reflection, by some other things.
>
> (1.2.51)

Under the guise of providing, in the shape of "thoughts of great value, worthy cogitations," a "mirror" to reflect his friend's "*hidden* worthiness," Cassius will bring him to see not a reality, an objective vision of his strength and weakness, but the "shadow" of the imperfectly understood desires which will finally bring him, not to the affirmation of his ideals, but to personal and public ruin.

Beneath these assertions of friendship and plain dealing, Cassius's approach to Brutus is fraught with calculation. Those of "the best respect in Rome" look to him for redress; as they groan beneath "this age's yoke," their desire is that "*noble* Brutus"—the adjective initiates a line of flattery which, precisely because it contains truth, will be particularly insidious—understood his own wishes and motives, "had his eyes." Brutus's first reaction is honest and true to character:

> Into what dangers would you lead me, Cassius,
> That you would have me seek into myself
> *For that which is not in me?*
>
> (1.2.63)

It is some time before he will speak so truly again. Meanwhile, it is Cassius's mission to undermine this candid self-estimate, replacing it by a false confidence which carries no inner conviction. Taking up the image of the mirror, he turns to his own ends the need for guidance which makes his friend so pliable to his purposes:

> since you know you cannot see yourself
> So well as by reflection, I your glass
> Will modestly discover to yourself
> That of yourself which you yet know not of.
>
> (1.2.67)

This is a dangerous proceeding, made the more so by the tendency, which the following exchanges reveal, for the two friends to vie with one another in setting up idealized images of themselves to minister to what is finally, beneath their poses of Roman virtue and public spirit, an intimate self-satisfaction. When Cassius denies that he is "a common laugher," "fawning" on men with the intention of later "scandalling" them, he is no doubt comparing himself, not altogether unjustly, with such as Antony and pointing to some true consequences of Caesar's exorbitant power; but, beneath the implied contrast, envy, the desire to debase what he has been unable to achieve, vitiates the judgment.

For Brutus, similarly, devotion to the public good expresses itself through assumption of that "honour" which was, more especially at this time, so variously in Shakespeare's mind:

> What is it that you would impart to me?
> If it be aught toward the general good,
> Set honour in one eye and death i' the other,
> And I will look on both indifferently.
>
> (1.2.84)

Though expressed with a more "philosophic" detachment, the spirit behind these words is akin to that which prompted Hotspur to his generous but useless sacrifice; and it reveals much the same tendency to replace the balance of judgment by simpler but more illusory certainties. As Brutus concludes, not without a touch of self-esteem,

> let the gods so speed me as I love
> The name of honour more than I fear death.
>
> (1.2.88)

It will be, perhaps, one of the lessons of Brutus's tragedy that the "names" of things, however noble and consoling in abstraction, are no substitute for a balanced consideration of their reality. "Honour" is the way of becoming a trap set for those who, like Brutus, fail to temper idealism with a proper measure of self-awareness.

The soliloquy in which Brutus finally arrives at his decision, and thereby makes the murder of Caesar possible, is so riddled with implicit contradictions that some students of the play have judged it incomprehensible. It is, however, thoroughly in character. Brutus, not himself an evil man, is about to perform an act which will release evil impulses whose true nature he persistently fails to grasp; the discrepancy between what he is and what he does is reflected in his recognizable effort to persuade himself, against convictions intimately present in his nature, that the resolve he is about to take is necessary and just. Had he been consistently the doctrinaire republican Cassius would have him be, the admitted fact that Caesar "would be crown'd" would have been, for him if not for Shakespeare and most of his contemporaries, a sufficient reason for his elimination. Brutus, however, as the play presents him, is no such thing, but rather a man who seeks in decisive action the confirmation of his own virtue, whose purposes are imposed upon him by those who play upon inconsistencies, weak spots in his own nature; and it is part of his tragedy that he cannot forget, much as he now desires to do so, that his intended victim is a human being and his friend. This situation bears fruit in his recognition, which a convinced republican would have found irrelevant, that he has as yet no valid *personal* reason for the deed he contemplates. "To speak truth of Caesar," he admits,

> I have not known when his affections sway'd
> More than his reason.
>
> (2.1.20)

"I know no personal cause to spurn at him": the admission is, for a man who sincerely values friendship, personal relationships, serious enough; but since another side of Brutus's nature craves abstract consistency, the wedding of high principle to effective action, he turns this recognition into an argument for clearing himself of dubious personal motives and seeks to place the burden of justification squarely upon an appeal to the "general" good.

The argument, inevitably, is pressed home with less than complete conviction. "How that *might* change his nature, there's the question," Brutus urges upon himself, in a strangely tentative attitude, only to recognize later that

> the quarrel
> Will bear no colour for the thing he is;
> (2.1.28)

but, since a contrary necessity urges him to conceal these doubts, calls upon him to assert a certainty which he is far from feeling, emphasis must be laid on a *possible*, an unproven danger:

> Fashion it thus; that what he is, augmented,
> Would run to these and these extremities.
> (2.1.30)

The vagueness, the readiness to "fashion it thus" in accordance with preconceptions in which observed reality has little part to play, is highly symptomatic. Brutus, precisely because the vacillation which has characterized his reactions since the beginning covers deep inner uncertainty, speaks to himself evasively in terms of specious "philosophical" commonplace—

> The abuse of greatness is when it disjoins
> Remorse from power . . .
> lowliness is young ambition's ladder—
> (2.1.18)

and takes refuge in an imposed ruthlessness:

> think him as a serpent's egg
> Which, hatched, would as his kind grow mischievous,
> And kill him in the shell.
> (2.1.32)

The tendency to cover lack of intimate consistency with a show of impersonal brutality belongs to Brutus's peculiar brand of theoretical idealism. It is part of the presentation of human contradiction, whose exposure is so close to the spirit of this play. Brutus seeks at this moment to resolve an intimate, tragic disharmony through an act of decision foreign to his nature; the confusion revealed in his own motives, and in his attitude to the world of external realities, is one that will follow him through the contradictions of his career to the final resolution of suicide.

Confronted with the conspirators he has agreed to lead, Brutus further reveals his true nature. In presenting him to them Cassius stresses his need to live up to the conception of himself which his ancestors and his "philosophy" had laid upon him. He suggests that, unlike these ancestors, Brutus is weak, indecisive; public opinion demands of him that "opinion" of himself which every true Roman wishes to share. Brutus, in reply, urges his new associates to confirm their dedication and seeks confidence in a rhetorical declaration of his own:

> do not stain
> The even virtue of our enterprize,
> Nor the insuppressive mettle of our spirits,
> To think that or our cause or our performance
> Did need an oath: when every drop of blood
> That every Roman bears, and nobly bears,
> Is guilty of a several bastardy
> If he do break the smallest particle
> Of any promise that hath pass'd from him.
>
> (2.1.132)

The best comment on this earnest but slightly self-conscious harangue is provided by the return, which at once follows, to practical considerations. Cassius and his friends wish to enrol the support of Cicero, whose reputation will "purchase us"—the verb is appropriately chosen—"a good opinion,"

> And buy men's voices to commend our deeds.

Since, however, it is Brutus's adhesion that all desire, it is enough for him to reject Cicero as incapable of "following" for all to agree that he should not be approached.

The basic weakness of the plot is more closely touched upon when Cassius urges that Mark Antony should die. Brutus's rejection of this advice is of very considerable interest as a further revelation of the kind of man he is. It combines an effort to be practical, revealed in the opening concession to expediency ("Our course will seem too bloody"), with failure to be so. It is finally the pose, the elevation of himself into a figure of magnanimous principle, that engages his emotions. The expression is not without a touch of the grotesque. "Let us be sacrificers, but not butchers, Caius," he urges, and follows up the plea with an unreal distinction between "the spirit of men" and their material "blood" which must so regrettably be shed:

> We all stand up against the spirit of Caesar,
> And in the spirit of men there is no blood!
> O, that we then could come by Caesar's spirit,
> And not dismember Caesar!
>
> (2.1.167)

The distinction no doubt answers in part to the desire to make credible Brutus's nobility in the face of the nature of the deed on which he has set himself. The difficulty, however, is turned into an asset, a revelation of character. Brutus the idealist is seen as one more example of that typical Shakespearean creation, the man who, willing an end, is ready to deceive himself concerning the means necessary to gain it. "Caesar must bleed for't," he recognizes, but covers the admission with futile and self-conscious posing:

> gentle friends,
> Let's kill him boldly, but not wrathfully:
> Let's carve him as a dish fit for the gods,
> Not hew him as a carcass fit for hounds:
> And let our hearts, as subtle masters do,
> Stir up their servants to an act of rage,
> And after seem to chide 'em.
>
> (2.1.171)

The speech points to the presence of a variety of motives in the process of decorating brutality with strained emotional expression. Addressing his future accomplices as "gentle friends," Brutus, in admitting the fact of bloody death, embroiders it with the far-fetched and finally absurd evocation of "a dish fit for the gods." The odd mixture of unpracticality and a certain unconscious cynicism is brought home forcibly in the description of the conspirators' hearts as "*subtle* masters" who, in rousing their "servant" feelings to a simulation, an "act of rage," *seem* after, for the purpose of obtaining public approval, "to chide them." "We shall be call'd purgers, not murderers": the reality, as so often occurs with men of Brutus's type, is disguised by a change of name, and this becomes the justification of a decision politically unwise, if humanly comprehensible, which will finally bring the conspiracy to ruin.

Such are the main elements which, converging, unite in the blow which strikes down Caesar in the central action of the play. The victim's last utterance, claiming the constancy of the "northern star," is the most theatrical of all his assertions of fixity. Just as his fall is about to stress his common humanity, he accentuates unnaturally the distance that separates him from other men:

> men are flesh and blood, and apprehensive;
> Yet in the number I do know but one
> That unassailable holds on his rank,
> Unshaked of motion;
>
> (3.1.67)

but already his own unsuspecting words—

> and that I am he
> Let me a little show it, even in this—
> (3.1.70)

amount to a plea, an appeal to the world to support him in this self-estimate. It finds its answer in the repeated stabs of Brutus and his associates, and in his fall at the foot of the effigy of Pompey, whom he himself formerly overthrew.

The fall is followed by a tense moment of silence, set against the gathering climax which has so splendidly preceded it. Immediately after this, the emotions so far concentrated upon Caesar's overpowering presence break out with the rising hysteria of libertarian sentiment. "Liberty! freedom! tyranny is dead!" cries Cinna; and even Brutus, after calling on those around him to maintain their calm, turns to a more emotional line of appeal:

> Stoop, Romans, stoop,
> And let us bathe our hands in Caesar's blood
> Up to the elbows, and besmear our swords;
> Then walk we forth, even to the market-place
> And, waving our red weapons o'er our heads,
> Let's all cry, "Peace, freedom, and liberty!"
> (3.1.105)

Here, if anywhere, and in the self-congratulatory exchanges that follow, a final comment on the true nature of conspiracy is unerringly made. The gap between profession and reality, the aspiration to freedom and the deed to which it has led, is remorselessly asserted in the insistence upon spilled blood: blood not, as in *Macbeth*, horrifyingly sticking to the assassin's hands, but lavish, free-flowing, answering to the strained emotions with which the murderers have sought to disguise, even from themselves the true nature of their crime.

In this charged emotional climate, Mark Antony—first through a messenger and then in his own person—cautiously feels his way to the centre of the stage. By the end of his exchange with Brutus, which culminates in a grotesque parody—"Let each man render me his bloody hand"—of the reconciliation which Caesar's assassin has so impossibly proposed, he knows that his position is stronger than he can have dared to hope. Left alone with his thoughts, his last speech in this scene is a further revelation of character. Couched in the facile rhetoric which comes so readily to him, it apostrophizes the dead Caesar as "thou bleeding piece of earth" and goes on to speak of "costly blood" and to characterize his wounds as "dumb mouths" and "ruby lips." In a world so fluent in feeling, where emotion swells in accordance with the forms of rhetoric, intensely rather than deeply, like the blood which issues from the wounds it contemplates, Antony's oratory is perfectly at home. It issues, however, in a vision of chaos. "All pity" shall be "chok'd" with "custom of fell deeds,"

> And Caesar's spirit ranging for revenge,
> With Ate by his side come hot from hell,
> Shall in these confines with a monarch's voice
> Cry "Havoc!" and let slip the dogs of war;
> That this foul deed shall smell above the earth
> With carrion men, groaning for burial.
>
> (3.1.270)

This conclusion to the first open revelation of his pent-up feelings carries with it an estimate of Antony's limitations as a moral being. His rhetoric pays itself with its own expression, represents emotional irresponsibility in one who can also calculate and use his rhetorical gifts for ends deliberately and cunningly conceived. The vision of chaos, far from appalling Antony, finally attracts him, answers to a necessity of his nature; and that is why his type of emotion, not less than Brutus's frigid assertions of principle, is to be seen less in its own right than as a fragment, a partial aspect of the unity which Caesar's death has destroyed in Rome. The end of this process is "carrion," self-destruction, death: that Antony, carried on the flow of words which reflects his emotional nature, can dwell with complacency on these dreadful realities is, by implication, an exposure of his most intimate motives.

The famous oration scene (3.2) is too familiar to call for analysis in detail. It shows a Brutus caught in the consequences of his own act, deprived—now that the mood of exaltation which accompanied him to it has passed—of the impulse to go further. Against him is set an Antony who, in the act of affirming himself as the adventurer and theatrical orator he is, is also the instrument by which the *truth* about murder emerges to the light of day. This clash of aims and temperament takes place before a background provided by a new element in the action: the Roman populace. The crowd has not hitherto played a decisive part in events, though its fickleness has been indicated more than once in the early scenes. It now makes the voice of its appetites heard in a more direct fashion, thereby showing from still another point of view the nature of the forces which Brutus and Cassius have so irresponsibly released from their normal restraints. At the end of the scene, as the mob moves off to burn and plunder, Antony's final comment is a revealing disclaimer of responsibility. "Now let it work": the orator, resting on his laurels, looks with satisfaction on his achievement, dwells with a certain pleasure on the chaos he has let loose:

> Mischief, thou art afoot,
> Take thou what course thou wilt.
>
> (3.2.265)

The final effect is a revelation of irresponsibility accompanied by sinister pleasure:

> Fortune is merry,
> And in this mood will give us anything.
>
> (3.2.271)

That, later on, she will assume other moods, ultimately less congenial to the speaker, remains to be seen. Meanwhile, the grim little episode

(3.3) of the destruction of Cinna the poet for a chance coincidence of name comes effectively to announce the brutality which will from now on so frequently preside over the course of events.

The unleashing of the Roman mob brings to an end the more dynamic part of the action. The last scenes of the tragedy exhibit the consequences of Caesar's murder in a spirit of notable detachment. They show a Rome divided by covert rivalries which can only end in the elimination of all but one of its contending factions and, after that elimination, in the restoration of unity under Octavius. Apart from this resolution, the personal tragedy of Brutus is rounded off in the self-inflicted death which is its logical conclusion.

It is important to note that this dispassionate evaluation falls impartially on both parties. As the fourth act opens, Antony and a notably frigid and noncommittal Octavius are seen in the company of Lepidus, contemplating the death of their relations and former friends without illusion and without feeling. The initial words of Antony, who has so recently exhibited himself in the forum as a man of sensibility, are "These many then shall die"; Octavius, typically passing from the general statement to its particular application, adds (turning to Lepidus) "Your brother too must die," and obtains his companion's assent:

> Upon condition Publius shall not live,
> Who is your sister's son, Mark Antony.
>
> (4.1.4)

The callousness of the exchange, the readiness to write off human lives by marks on paper, is rounded off by Antony's complacent rejoinder: "He shall not live; look, with a spot I damn him." The final suggestion that the will, which Antony has so recently used to stir up mob emotion in the name of generosity, should be studied to determine "How to cut off some charge in legacies" adds a revealing touch of parsimony to the display of cynicism in action.

The world which is to replace that formerly dominated by Caesar is indeed mean, petty, and dangerous. The triumvirs are already engaged in the first stages of a ruthless struggle for power. As soon as Lepidus has been dispatched for the will, Antony refers disparagingly to him ("a slight unmeritable man"; "meet to be sent on errands") and proposes his elimination. Octavius, whose moment is still to come, bides his time ("he is a tried and valiant soldier") and is answered by Antony with a further display of cynicism. "So is

my horse, Octavius"; with Lepidus thus removed from consideration, the two leaders return to discussion of the "great things" in
which their own future is involved. The last words of the scene,
spoken by Octavius, stress the insecurity that now surrounds the
entire political future:

> some that smile have in their hearts, I fear,
> Millions of mischiefs.
>
> (4.1.50)

Such is the world which has survived Caesar, and in which his
avengers are fated to move.

On the other side the circumstances of Caesar's enemies, as they
are shown in the process of coming to terms with their real as distinct
from their rhetorical selves, answer to a conception which is, in its
accepted pessimism, finally similar. In them, division and self-doubt
replace the cynical manoeuvres of their foes. Cassius, no longer the
ardent friend of the early scenes, whom the prospect of action united
(perhaps, in the last analysis, spuriously) to a colleague whom interest
also demanded as his associate, now salutes that associate with distant
correctness, no longer shows

> such free and friendly conference,
> As he hath used of old.
>
> (4.2.17)

Brutus's reaction is heavy with the sense of fatality. Lucilius has
described "a hot friend cooling," and the process by which love
begins "to sicken and decay" has its symptoms in "an enforced
ceremony." The wish of Brutus to maintain "plain and simple faith"
is at once moving and strangely inadequate. It springs from his most
deeply held theoretical conception of life, in the absence of which
his integrity, his belief in himself and in the purity of his motives,
must founder; but it runs against the nature of things as determined
by the course of action in which he has compromised his honesty.
Against the background of advancing armies we feel already the
"sinking at the trial" which, proceeding from adverse external realities, mirrors inner dejection.

The motives behind this discussion are, from the first, of some
complexity. Cassius, rushing typically into the void which opens
before him, complains that he has been "wrong'd"; but it is clear

from his explanation that the wrong—an accusation of connivance in accepting bribes—has been inflicted in a dubious context. Brutus, indeed, having made his point in a tone of moral superiority—"You wrong'd yourself to write in such a case"—cannot refrain from rubbing salt into the wound. By accusing Cassius of "an itching palm," he rouses the impetuous self-respect of his friend to violent protest:

> You know that you are Brutus that speaks this,
> Or, by the gods, this speech were else your last;
>
> (4.3.13)

and there is a touch of insensitivity in the responding reference to "chastisement" which leaves Cassius speechless in its implication of lofty superiority. The two characters, so precariously united against Caesar, are seen to be perfectly designed to exasperate one another to the limits of endurance.

As the gap between them widens, Brutus is led to recall the integrity which inspired their actions: "Did not great Caesar bleed for justice' sake?" This thought, contrasted with the sad reality of the present, leads him to back his reproof with a further gesture towards the idealism of the past:

> What, shall one of us
> That struck the foremost man of all this world
> But for supporting robbers, shall we now
> Contaminate our fingers with base bribes,
> And sell the mighty space of our large honours
> For so much trash as may be grasped thus?
>
> (4.3.21)

The gesture is ample, noble, and yet it covers weakness. As always, Brutus is taking refuge in a satisfactory picture of himself as one who has dared, for "honour" alone, to lead and inspire a conspiracy that overthrew "the foremost man of all this world"; but where disinterest ends and egoism, the need to live up to an ennobling vision of his own motives, begins, we might be hard put to decide.

Whatever the truth about Brutus's purity (and no simple judgment would be appropriate) his attitude could not be more precisely calculated to rub the raw edges of Cassius's sense of inferiority. As Brutus ceases, he describes what he has heard as a "baiting" of himself and utters the ominous warning: "I'll not endure it." His touchy self-respect has been offended, and now responds by appealing to his superior experience:

> I am a soldier, I,
> Older in practice, abler than yourself
> To make conditions.
>
> (4.3.30)

The repetition of "I" indicates the nature of the wound inflicted upon Cassius's own type of egoism. That of Brutus, though more complex, is not less strong. It impels him, where tact would have passed over the burning issue, to exasperate his companion further by contemptuous denial. "You are not, Cassius." "I am." "I say you are not": the result is to create an ugly wrangle in which the last shreds of self-respect seem likely to be swallowed up. At the culminating moment, Cassius's threatening "tempt me no further" is matched by the infuriating superiority of "Away, slight man!" and by the final insult:

> Hear me, for I will speak.
> Must I give way and room to your rash choler?
>
> (4.3.38)

At this moment, the realities of character which underlie the previous affirmations of constancy and devotion to principle are revealed for what they are. The rest of the scene is devoted to working them out fully, and to an attempt to cover them up in the interests of a cause already lost.

At first, however, it is not a matter of covering up, but of adding further irritation to Cassius's open wound. In this Brutus, by a trait which links curiously with his self-conscious idealism, but which is not on reflection incompatible with it, is a master. "Must I endure all this?" Cassius cries, as though demanding clemency, and receives the bitter exasperation of the insult—"All this! ay more! Fret till your proud heart break"—and the contemptuous dismissal that follows:

> Go show your slaves how choleric you are,
> And make your bondmen tremble!
>
> (4.3.43)

The rest of the speech, so true to the frigid egoism of the man "armed strong in honesty," rises to a final, almost sadistic determination to inflict humiliation:

> By the gods,
> You shall digest the venom of your spleen,
> Though it do split you; for from this day forth,
> I'll use you for my mirth, yea, for my laughter,
> When you are waspish.
>
> (4.3.46)

The lines are rich in inflection, in the varied revelation of character. There is pleasure in inflicting humiliation, moral callousness, and contempt, together with a bitter pleasure in true characterization in the final description of Cassius as "waspish." The fact is that the element of egoism present from the first beneath Brutus's noble façade is coming to the surface under the stress of his growing awareness of standing intolerably in a false situation. The effect of this outburst, though palliated, can never be undone; and Cassius's broken reply, "Is it come to this?" clearly involves a glance back to the idealistic unity of purpose in which Caesar's murder was carried out and which is now being revealed in so unflattering a light.

The healing of this breach and the return to at least the appearance of unity are accomplished with no small tact. The conspirators, seeing the abyss opening at their feet, draw back in horror. Both, we may feel, are moved beneath the surface of their reproaches by a sense that it is their own past, their capacity for continued belief in their moral dignity, which they are in reality placing in jeopardy; and when Cassius breaks into further reproach, self-exhibition is subtly combined with a true sense of personal betrayal. "Cassius is a-weary of the world": here it may seem that a conscious appeal to emotion prevails, but the following phrases surely strike a valid note in their criticism of Brutus's frigid moralizing:

> Hated by one he loves; braved by his brother!
> Check'd like a bondman; all his faults observed,
> Set in a note-book, learn'd, and conn'd by rote,
> To cast into my teeth.
>
> (4.3.95)

Brutus, no doubt realizing that he has gone too far, meets this outburst, which culminates in Cassius's offer of his dagger, with a genuine attempt to reduce the tension. He is, however, characteristically clumsy in his effort to adjust his words to a new mood. His phrase "Be angry when you will, it shall have scope" sounds stiffly, rather

like the humouring of a self-willed child; men such as Brutus do not easily descend from the pedestal on which their lives are based. Beneath the clumsiness, however, there is now revealed a deep unhappiness, the immediate cause of which is still being held back from us:

> O Cassius, you are yoked with a lamb,
> That carries anger as the flint bears fire,
> Who, much enforced, shows a hasty spark,
> And straight is cold again.
>
> (4.3.109)

The reference to feeling hardly struck as from a flinty surface, an innate coldness, reveals tellingly the diffidence, the emotional clumsiness, which is part of the character; and the sincerity of the revelation opens the way to a rueful, disillusioned reconciliation. The impression left by the whole exchange is one of the cooling embers of a passion doomed to extinction, but surviving, at least for the moment, the death of the original flame.

The immediate reason for Brutus's state, however, and for much that has gone before, has so far been held back by an admirable stroke of dramatic tact. It is now revealed. After calling for a bowl of wine, symbol—as it were—of harmony between friends, he meets Cassius's wondering comment "I did not think you could have been so angry" and the reproof of "Of your philosophy you make no use" with his simple revelation: "No man bears sorrow better: Portia is dead." The disclosure, followed by an admirably brief and tense exchange of phrases—

> —Portia is dead.
> —Ha, Portia!
> —She is dead—
>
> (4.3.146)

gives a centre of stillness to the bitter exchanges that have gone before. From this heart of silence, Cassius's emotion speaks in a new, transformed tone: "How 'scaped I killing when I cross'd you so?" and backs it with the almost choric quality of his following exclamation: "O insupportable and touching loss!"

The revelation is rounded off with the recovery by Brutus of his Stoic mask: "Speak no more of her!" If the "philosopher" in him dictates this assertion of emotional control, the husband's affection warns him not to give voice to a feeling which, once expressed,

might shatter all containing limits. The hidden cause of emotional stress having been thus revealed, the bowl of wine is brought in, and in it Brutus pledges himself to "bury all unkindness," receiving in return the fullness of Cassius's answering pledge:

> My heart is thirsty for that noble pledge.
> Fill, Lucius, till the wine o'erswell the cup;
> I cannot drink too much of Brutus' love.
>
> (4.3.159)

The reconciliation takes place under the shadow of tragedy. It cannot be a restoration of the original relationship, now irretrievably flawed by past choices; but, in spite of this, the human content is there, beyond all the purposes of political realism, and it rounds off suitably the issues so dramatically represented in what is, in some respects, the most interesting scene of the play.

The last stages of the tragedy represent the winding-up of the action in accordance with its underlying constants. The defeated Romans fall on their swords in a show of Stoic resolution, because no other choice is left open to them, and the victors turn away from the field "to part the glory of this happy day." As we follow these episodes to their conclusion, we cannot help feeling that something of the shadow of the Greek heroes in *Troilus and Cressida*, written possibly at a time not very far distant, already lies over them. Cassius commits suicide in an error caused by his own shortsightedness (as Titinius says: "Alas, thou hast misconstrued everything!"), and the cold, practical Octavius is shown on the other side as reacting against the tutelage of Antony, who has made his victory possible and whom he will soon be ready to discard. With all his flaws, which have been so uncompromisingly revealed in the course of the play, Brutus is the only character who emerges with some measure of genuine personal stature. His last farewell rises, in contrast with so much that surrounds it, to the dignity of tragic assertion. "Countrymen," he says, addressing through his remaining followers Rome and posterity:

> My heart doth joy that yet in all my life
> I found no man but he was true to me.
> I shall have glory by this losing day,
> More than Octavius and Mark Antony
> By this vile conquest shall attain unto.
>
> (5.5.34)

Once more it is important to avoid any simple reaction to the mood so expressed. The speech is truly noble, but is also an effort made by the speaker, in the absence of more solid ground for satisfaction, to encourage himself on the threshold of the annihilation which he has, after all, brought upon himself, and perhaps even obscurely come to desire.

The mood is, in any case, neither false nor triumphant, implies rather an acceptance of the end Brutus has come to see as inevitable, involved in the entire logic of his own past, and which he now approaches with a certain nostalgic craving for the dark:

> Night hangs upon mine eyes; my bones would rest,
> That have but labour'd to attain this hour.
>
> (5.5.41)

In this mood of self-awareness, and snatching some crumb of comfort from the fact that Strato, the instrument of his release, is "a fellow of a good report," he dies in a mood akin to expiation:

> Caesar, now be still;
> I kill'd not thee with half so good a will.
>
> (5.5.50)

In this admission, the whole contradictory nature of the enterprise to which Brutus so perversely forced himself in the name of humanity is gathered up in the prelude to a last act of self-annihilating resolve.

When Octavius enters to wind up the action with Antony, Strato is able to turn on Messala, now a bondman to the conqueror, with an assertion of the freedom that Brutus has found in death:

> Brutus only overcame himself,
> And no man else hath honour by his death.
>
> (5.5.56)

For all his devotion, however, he is ready to follow Messala by joining the conquerer; the world of rhetorical aspiration and that of practical reality rarely run parallel. The contrast between personal integrity and the way of a world from which, we have good reason to believe, it will be increasingly exiled, is implicit in Antony's epitaph, in which he justifiably glorifies Brutus's personal qualities—

> This was the noblest Roman of them all—
>
> (5.5.68)

without concealing the "envy" which surrounded this nobility and used its inherent flaws for ends of its own. Octavius, having made the victor's appropriate gesture of generosity, now that generosity can no longer endanger his triumph, turns away with his companion to enjoy the "glory" they have won. The results to which this sharing of the fruits of victory will lead are to be the theme for another play.

Ritual and *Julius Caesar*

Lawrence Danson

In *Julius Caesar* we find, more starkly and simply than in *Hamlet,* those problems of communication and expression, those confusions linguistic and ritualistic, which mark the world of the tragedies. The play opens with the sort of apparently expository scene in which Shakespeare actually gives us the major action of the play in miniature. Flavius and Marullus, the tribunes, can barely understand the punning language of the commoners; had they the wit, they might exclaim with Hamlet, "Equivocation will undo us." It is ostensibly broad daylight in Rome, but the situation is dreamlike; for although the language which the two classes speak is phonetically identical, it is, semantically, two separate languages. The cobbler's language, though it sounds like the tribunes', is (to the tribunes) a sort of inexplicable dumb show.

And as with words, so with gestures; the certainties of ceremonial order are as lacking in Rome, as are the certainties of the verbal language. The commoners present an anomaly to the tribunes simply by walking "Upon a labouring day without the sign / Of [their] profession." To the commoners it is a "holiday," to the tribunes (although in fact it is the Feast of Lupercal), a "labouring day." The commoners have planned an observance of Caesar's triumph—itself, to the tribunes, no triumph but rather a perversion of Roman

From *Tragic Alphabet: Shakespeare's Drama of Language.* © 1974 by Yale University. Yale University Press, 1974.

order—but the tribunes send the "idle creatures" off to perform a
quite different ceremony:

> Go, go, good countrymen, and for this fault
> Assemble all the poor men of our sort;
> Draw them to Tiber banks, and weep your tears
> Into the channel, till the lowest stream
> Do kiss the most exalted shores of all.
>
> (1.1.57)

Thus, in a Rome where each man's language is foreign to the
next, ritual gestures are converted into their opposites; confusion in
the state's symbolic system makes every action perilously ambiguous. The tribunes, having turned the commoners' planned ritual into
its opposite, go off bravely to make their own gesture, to "Disrobe
the images" of Caesar; but shortly we learn that they have actually
been made to play parts in a bloodier ritual (one which, as we shall
see, becomes increasingly common in the play). And when, in a later
scene, we find Brutus deciding upon *his* proper gesture, the confusions of this first scene should recur to us.

The second scene again opens with mention of specifically ritual
observance, as Caesar bids Calphurnia stand in Antony's way to
receive the touch which will "Shake off [her] sterile curse" (1.2.9).
Perhaps Shakespeare intends to satirize Caesar's superstitiousness; at
least we can say that Calphurnia's sterility and the fructifying touch
introduce the question, what sort of ritual can assure (political) succession in Rome? Directly, the Soothsayer steps forth, warning Caesar, "Beware the ides of March." But this communication is not
understood: "He is a dreamer; Let us leave him. Pass" (1.2.24).

What follows, when Caesar and his train have passed off the
stage leaving Brutus and Cassius behind, is an enactment—virtually
an iconic presentation—of the linguistic problem. More clearly even
than the first scene, this scene gives us the picture of Rome as a place
where words and rituals have dangerously lost their conventional
meanings. As Cassius begins to feel out Brutus about the conspiracy—telling him of Rome's danger and wishes, of Caesar's pitiful
mortality, of Brutus's republican heritage—their conversation is
punctuated by shouts from offstage, shouts at whose meaning they
can only guess. (The situation brings to mind the one in *Hamlet*
when the men on the battlements question each other about the
strange new customs in Denmark.)

Casca, an eyewitness to the ritual in the marketplace, finally arrives to be their interpreter; but even he has understood imperfectly. Caesar (he says) has been offered the crown, but

> I can as well be hang'd as tell the manner of it: it was mere
> foolery; I did not mark it. I saw Mark Antony offer him
> a crown—yet 'twas not a crown neither, 'twas one of these
> coronets.
>
> (1.2.234)

Caesar refused the crown, but Casca suspects "he would fain have had it." "The rabblement hooted," and Casear "swooned and fell down at" the stench. As for the rest, Cicero spoke, but again the language problem intervened: "He spoke Greek." There is other news: "Marullus and Flavius, for pulling scarfs off Caesar's images, are put to silence." And, "There was more foolery yet, if I could remember it" (1.2.286).

The dramatic point of it all lies not so much in the conflict between republican and monarchical principles, as in the sheer confusion of the reported and overheard scene. It is all hooting and clapping and uttering of bad breath, swooning, foaming at the mouth, and speaking Greek. Cascas's cynical tone is well suited to the occasion, for the farcical charade of the crown-ritual, with Caesar's refusal and Antony's urging, is itself a cynical manipulation. The crowd clapped and hissed "as they use to do the players in the theatre" (1.2.260)—and rightly so.

These two opening scenes give us the world in which Brutus is to undertake his great gesture. When we next see Brutus, his decision is made: "It must be by his death" (2.1.10). Behind Brutus's decision is that linguistic and ceremonial confusion which is comic in the case of the commoners and sinister in the case of Caesar's crown-ritual. The innovations in Rome's ceremonial order give evidence to Brutus for the necessity of his gesture. But those same innovations, attesting to a failure in Rome's basic linguistic situation, also make it most probable that his gesture will fail. Brutus is not unlike Hamlet: he is a man called upon to make an expressive gesture in a world where the commensurate values necessary to expression are lacking. The killing of Caesar, despite the honorable intentions that are within Brutus and passing show, will thus be only one more ambiguous, misunderstood action in a world where no action can have an assured value. Brutus's grand expression might as well be Greek in this Roman world.

Brutus's position is not unlike Hamlet's, but he does not see what Hamlet sees. Indeed, he does not even see as much as his fellow conspirators do. To Cassius, the dreadful and unnatural storm over Rome reflects "the work we have in hand" (1.3.129); to the thoughtful Casca, the confusion in the heavens is an aspect of the confusion in Rome. But Brutus is, typically, unmoved by the storm, and calmly makes use of its strange light to view the situation: "The exhalations, whizzing in the air, / Give so much light that I may read by them" (2.1.44). And what he reads by this deceptive light is as ambiguous as the shouts of the crowd at the crown-ritual: the paper bears temptations slipped into his study by the conspirators, words that mislead and may betray. On the basis of this mysterious communication, revealed by a taper's dim light and the unnatural "exhalations" above, Brutus determines to "speak and strike." Every sign is misinterpreted by Brutus; and the world that seems to him to make a clear demand for words and gestures is in fact a world where words are equivocal and where gestures quickly wither into their opposites.

The situation, as I have so far described it, forces upon us the question critics of the play have most frequently debated: who is the play's hero? A simple enough question, it would seem: the title tells us that this is *The Tragedy of Julius Caesar*. But that answer only serves to show the actual complexity of the question, for if Caesar (who is, after all, dead by the middle of the play) is to this play what, say, Hamlet is to his, then *Julius Caesar* is, structurally at least, a most peculiar tragedy. The question of the hero—and a glance at the critical literature shows that the position is indeed questionable—bears upon fundamental matters of meaning and structure.

Now it is a curious fact about Shakespeare's plays (and, to an extent, about all drama) that the questions the critics ask have a way of duplicating the questions the characters ask, as though the playwright had done his best to make all criticism redundant. As if the play were not enough, nor the characters sufficient unto their conflicts, the critical audience continues to fight the same fights and ask the same questions the characters in the play do. Of *Julius Caesar*, as I have said, the question we most often ask concerns the play's hero: Caesar or Brutus? I have not bothered to tally the choices; for our purposes it is more interesting to notice the mode of critical procedure and the way in which it tends to imitate the actions of the characters in the play. Both critics and characters tend to choose sides in their

respective conflicts on the bases of political prejudice and evaluations
of moral rectitude. Since the moral and political issues in *Julius Caesar*
are themselves eternally moot, it is not surprising that the critical
debate continues unresolved.

About Caesar, for instance: if we try to make our determination
of herohood on the basis of Caesar's moral stature, we are doing
precisely what the characters do; and we find, I think, that he becomes
for us what he is for Shakespeare's Romans, less a man than the
object of men's speculations. Caesar is the Colossus whose legs we
may peep about but whom we can never know; characters and audience alike peep assiduously, each giving us a partial view which
simply will not accord with any other. Within the play, Caesar is
virtually constituted of the guesses made about him: Casca's rude
mockery, Cassius's sneers, Brutus's composite portrait of the present
Caesar (against whom he knows no wrong) and the dangerous serpent of the future, Antony's passionate defense, the mob's fickle love
and hate: these are the guesses, and contradictory as they are, they
give us the Caesar of the play—and of the play's critics.

Of Caesar's, or for that matter of Brutus's, moral status we can
have little more certain knowledge than the characters themselves
have. What we are in a privileged position to know is the *structure*
of the play: the characters' prison, the play's encompassing form, is
our revelation. What I propose to do, therefore, is to look at the
implicit answer Brutus gives (through his actions) to the question,
who is the play's tragic hero?, and compare that answer to the answer
revealed by the play's unfolding structure.

Everything Brutus does (until the collapse of the conspiracy) is
calculated to justify the title of the play, to make it indeed *The Tragedy
of Julius Caesar*. As we watch Brutus directing the conspiracy, we
watch a man plotting a typical Shakespearean tragedy; and it is crucial
to the success of his plot that Caesar indeed be its hero-victim. The
assassination, as Brutus conceives it, must have all the solemnity and
finality of a tragic play. The wonder of the spectacle must, as in
tragedy, join the audience (both within and without the play) into a
community of assent to the deed. For his part, Brutus is content
with a necessary secondary role, the mere agent of the hero's down-
fall—a kind of Laertes, or a more virtuous Aufidius to Caesar's
Coriolanus.

But of course Brutus's plot (in both senses of the word) is a
failure. The withholding of assent by the audience (again, both within
and without the play) proves his failure more conclusively than do

moral or political considerations. Brutus misunderstands the language of Rome; he misinterprets all the signs both cosmic and earthly; and the furthest reach of his failure is his failure to grasp, until the very end, the destined shape of his play. Brutus's plot is a failure, but by attending to the direction he tries to give it we can find, ironically, a clear anatomy of the typical tragic action.

Brutus makes his decision and in act 2, scene 1 he meets with the conspirators. Decius puts the question, "Shall no man else be touch'd but only Caesar?" Cassius, whose concerns are wholly practical, urges Antony's death. But Brutus demurs: the assassination as he conceives it has a symbolic dimension as important as its practical dimension; and although Brutus is not able to keep the two clearly separated (he opposes Antony's death partly out of concern for the deed's appearance "to the common eyes") he is clear about the need for a single sacrificial victim. His emphasis on sacrifice indicates the ritual shape Brutus hopes to give the assassination:

> Let's be sacrificers, but not butchers, Caius.
> We all stand up against the spirit of Caesar,
> And in the spirit of men there is no blood.
> O that we then could come by Caesar's spirit,
> And not dismember Caesar! But, alas,
> Caesar must bleed for it! And, gentle friends,
> Let's kill him boldly, but not wrathfully;
> Let's carve him as a dish fit for the gods,
> Not hew him as a carcass fit for hounds.
>
> . . . .
>
> We shall be call'd purgers, but not murderers.
>
> (2.1.166, 180)

The "sacrifice" must not be confused with murder, with mere butchery. The name of the deed becomes all important, indicating the distance between a gratuitous, essentially meaningless gesture, and a sanctioned, efficacious, unambiguous ritual.

But Brutus's speech, with a fine irony, betrays his own fatal confusion. "In the spirit of men there is no blood," but in this spirit—this symbol, this embodiment of Caesarism—there is, "alas," as much blood as Lady Macbeth will find in Duncan. Whatever we may feel about Brutus's political intentions, we must acknowledge a failure which has, it seems to me, as much to do with logic and language as with politics: Brutus is simply unclear about the difference between symbols and men. And his confusion, which leads to the semantic confusion between "murder" and "sacrifice," and between meaningless gestures and sanctioned ritual, is the central case of something we see at every social level in Rome. The assassination Brutus plans as a means of purging Rome dwindles to just more of the old ambiguous words and empty gestures. The assassination loses its intended meaning as surely as the commoners' celebration did in scene 1.

The assassination is surrounded by Brutus with all the rhetoric and actions of a sacrificial rite. It becomes ritually and literally a bloodbath, as Brutus bids,

> Stoop, Romans, stoop,
> And let us bathe our hands in Caesar's blood
> Up to the elbows, and besmear our swords.
>
> (3.1.106)

Even the disastrous decision to allow Antony to address the mob arises from Brutus's concern that "Caesar shall / Have all true rites and lawful ceremonies" (3.1.241). In Brutus's plot, where Caesar is the hero-victim whose death brings tragedy's "calm of mind, all passion spent," no one, not even Antony, should be left out of the ceremonious finale. With the conspirators' ritualized bloodbath, indeed, the implied metaphor of the assassination-as-drama becomes explicit—if also horribly ironic:

> CASSIUS: Stoop then, and wash. How many ages hence
>   Shall this our lofty scene be acted over
>   In states unborn and accents yet unknown!
> BRUTUS: How many times shall Caesar bleed in sport.
>
> (3.1.112)

Trapped in their bloody pageant, these histrionic conspirators cannot see what, in the terms they themselves suggest, is the most important point of all: this lofty scene occurs, not at the end, but in the middle of a tragic play.

Brutus's plot is not Shakespeare's; and immediately after the conspirators have acted out what should be the denouement of their tragic play, the actual shape of the play (the one they cannot see as such) begins to make itself clear. Antony, pointedly recalling Brutus's distinction between "sacrificers" and "butchers," says to the slaughtered symbol of tyranny, "O, pardon me, thou bleeding piece of

earth, / That I am meek and gentle with these butchers!" (3.1.255),
and announces the further course of the action:

> And Caesar's spirit, ranging for revenge,
> With Ate by his side come hot from hell,
> Shall in these confines with a monarch's voice
> Cry "Havoc!" and let slip the dogs of war,
> That this foul deed shall smell above the earth
> With carrion men, groaning for burial.
>
> (3.1.271)

Brutus's revolutionary gesture, which was intended to bring to birth
a stabler order, has been (in an esthetic as well as a political sense)
premature. His ritual has failed, and now, as Caesar's spirit ranges
for revenge (for there *is* blood in the spirits of men), it still remains
for the proper ritual to be found. Now Brutus will at last assume
his proper role: Brutus must be our tragic hero.

Of course he does his best to deny that role. His stoicism—the
coolness, for instance, with which he dismisses Caesar's ghost:
"Why, I will see thee at Philippi, then" (4.3.284)—is hardly what
we expect of the grandly suffering tragic hero. Still, it is to Brutus
that we owe one of the finest descriptions of the peculiar moment
in time occupied by a Shakespearean tragedy:

> Since Cassius first did whet me against Caesar,
> I have not slept.
> Between the acting of a dreadful thing
> And the first motion, all the interim is
> Like a phantasma or a hideous dream.
> The Genius and the mortal instruments
> Are then in council; and the state of man,
> Like to a little kingdom, suffers then
> The nature of an insurrection.
>
> (2.1.61)

The moment is suspended, irresolute, but charged with the energy
to complete itself. The separation of "acting" from "first motion,"
of "Genius" from "mortal instruments," is an intolerable state—the
measure of it is the insomnia—which demands resolution. In *Macbeth*
we will see this moment protracted and anatomized; it is the tragic
moment, and Brutus, for all his Roman calm, must pass through it
to its necessary completion.

The acting of the "dreadful thing"—or, rather, what Brutus thinks is the dreadful thing, Caesar's death—does not bring the promised end; that is made immediately clear. Antony's funeral oration shows that Brutus's grand gesture has changed little. Antony easily converts Brutus's sacrifice into murder. In Rome (as in Elsinore) men's actions merely "seem," and Antony can shift the intended meaning of Brutus's action as easily as the tribunes had changed the intended meaning of the commoner's actions in act 1, scene 1. Antony can use virtually the same words as the conspirators—he can still call Brutus an "honourable man" and Caesar "ambitious"—and yet make condemnation of approval and approval of condemnation. Even after the revolutionary moment of Ceasar's death, this Rome is all of a piece: a volatile mob, empty ceremonies, and a language as problematic as the reality it describes.

Even names are problematic here. It was with names that Cassius first went to work on Brutus:

> "Brutus" and "Caesar." What should be in that
>   "Caesar"?
> Why should that name be sounded more than
>   yours?
> Write them together: yours is as fair a name.
> Sound them: it doth become the mouth as
>   well.
> Weigh them: it is as heavy. Conjure with 'em:
> "Brutus" will start a spirit as soon as "Caesar."
>
>   (1.2.142)

Cassius's contemptuous nominalism reminds one of Edmund in *King Lear*, who also thinks that one name—that of "bastard," for instance—is as good as any other. Names, to Cassius and Edmund, are conventional signs having reference to no absolute value, and they may be manipulated at will.

In his funeral oration, Antony also plays freely with names; and with the repetition of those two names "Brutus" and "Caesar" he does indeed conjure a spirit. It is the spirit of riot, of random violence, and its first victim (with a grotesque appropriateness) is a poet and a name:

> THIRD PLEBIAN: Your name sir, truly.
> CINNA: Truly, my name is Cinna.

FIRST PLEBIAN: Tear him to pieces; he's a conspirator!
CINNA: I am Cinna the poet, I am Cinna the poet.
FOURTH PLEBIAN: Tear him for his bad verses, tear him for
    his bad verses!
CINNA: I am not Cinna the conspirator.
FOURTH PLEBIAN: It is no matter, his name's Cinna; pluck
    but his name out of his heart, and turn him going.
THIRD PLEBIAN: Tear him, tear him!

                                    (3.3.26)

"Pluck but his name out of his heart, and turn him going": it is like
Brutus's impossible, "And in the spirit of men there is no blood."
Again, it is the confusion between symbol and reality, between the
abstract name and the blood-filled man who bears it. Poets, whose
genius it is to mediate symbol and reality and to find the appropriate
name to match all things, generally have rough going in *Julius Caesar*.
Brutus the liberator shows how he has insensibly aged into a figure
indistinguishable from the tyrant when he dismisses a peacemaking
poet with a curt, "What should the wars do with these jigging fools?"
(4.3.135). And Caesar, too, had rebuffed a poetical soothsayer.

    The gratuitous murder of Cinna the poet reflects ironically upon
the murder of Caesar. The poet's rending at the hands of the mob
is unreasonable, based solely on a confusion of identities (of names,
words), and while it bears some resemblance to the sacrifice of a
scapegoat figure, it is really no sacrifice at all but unsanctioned murder. Caesar's death, similarly, was undertaken as a sacrificial gesture,
but quickly became identified with plain butchery. In the mirror of
the Cinna episode the assassination is seen as only one case in a series
of perverted rituals—a series that runs with increasing frequency
now, until the proper victim and the proper form are at last found.

    Immediately following the murder of Cinna we see the new
triumvirate picking the names of its victims. The death of Caesar
has released the motive force behind the tragedy, and that force runs
unchecked now until the final sacrifice at Philippi. From the very
first scene of the play we have witnessed ritual gestures that wither
into meaninglessness; with the conspiracy and Caesar's death, we
become aware of sacrifice as the particular ritual toward which the
world of the play is struggling: the series of mistaken rituals becomes
a series of mistaken sacrifices, culminating at Philippi.

The wrong sacrifice, the wrong victim: the play offers an astonishing gallery of them. It has been noticed that all of the major characters implicate themselves in this central action:

> Each character in the political quartet in turn makes a similar kind of theatrical gesture implying the sacrifice of his own life: to top his refusal of the crown, Caesar offers the Roman mob his throat to cut; Brutus shows the same people that he has a dagger ready for himself, in case Rome should need his death; with half-hidden irony, Antony begs his death of the conspirators; and in the quarrel scene, Cassius gives his "naked breast" for Brutus to strike.
>
> (Adrien Bonjour, *The Structure of* Julius Caesar)

The idea of sacrifice is imagistically linked to the idea of hunters and the hunted. Caesar, says Antony, lies "like a deer strucken by many princes" (3.1.210). The ruthless Octavius feels, improbably enough, that he is "at the stake, / And bay'd about with many enemies" (4.1.48). But it was the conspirators themselves who first suggested the analogy between sacrifice and hunting: their blood-bathing ceremony suggests (as Antony makes explicit) the actions of a hunter with his first kill. And finally, appropriately, the sacrifice-hunting imagery fastens on Brutus: "Our enemies have beat us to the pit" (5.5.23).

From a slightly different perspective, the final scenes at Philippi might be a comedy of errors. Military bungles and mistaken identities follow quickly on each other's heels; the number of suicides, especially, seems excessive. Of the suicide of Titinius, a relatively minor character, Granville-Barker asks, "why, with two suicides to provide for, Shakespeare burdened himself with this third?" The answer to his question, and the explanation for the apparent excesses generally, must be found, I believe, in the context of false sacrifice throughout the play. Caesar's death was one such false sacrifice; Cinna the poet's a horrible mistake; the political murders by the triumvirate continued the chain; and now Cassius sacrifices himself on the basis of a mistake, while Titinius follows out of loyalty to the dead Cassius. Brutus embarked on the conspiracy because he misinterpreted the confused signs in, and above, Rome; the intended meaning of his own gesture was in turn subverted by Antony and the mob. And now Cassius has misinterpreted the signs: friendly troops are mistaken for hostile,

their shouts of joy are not understood; thus "Caesar, thou art re-
veng'd," as Cassius dies, in error, "Even with the sword that kill'd
thee" (5.3.45). And, because Cassius has "misconstrued every thing"
(as Titinius puts it [5.3.84]), Titinius now dies, bidding, "Brutus,
come apace."

Titinius places a garland on the dead Cassius before he dies
himself; and Brutus, entering when both are dead, pronounces a
solemn epitaph:

> Are yet two Romans living such as these?
> The last of all the Romans, fare thee well!
> It is impossible that ever Rome
> Should breed thy fellow. Friends, I owe more tears
> To this dead man than you shall see me pay.
> I shall find time, Cassius, I shall find time.
>
> (5.3.98)

The words and the actions form an appropriate tragic device of
wonder—but this is no more the end than it was when Brutus spoke
an epitaph for Caesar. The death of Cassius is still not the proper
sacrifice, and the play has still to reach its culminating ritual.

At Philippi, Brutus at last accepts his role. Against the wishes
of Cassius, Brutus insists upon meeting the enemy even before (as
the enemy puts it), "we do demand of them." The ghost of Caesar
has appeared and Brutus has accepted its portent: "I know my hour
is come"(5.5.20). Most significant in Brutus's final speeches is their
tone of acceptance:

> Countrymen,
> My heart doth joy that yet in all my life,
> I found no man but he was true to me.
> I shall have glory by this losing day,
> More than Octavius and Mark Antony
> By this vile conquest shall attain unto.
> So fare you well at once; for Brutus' tongue
> Hath almost ended his life's history.
> Night hangs upon mine eyes; my bones would rest,
> That have but labour'd to attain this hour.
>
> (5.5.33)

The expressed idea of the glorious defeat is an authentic sign of
Shakespearean tragedy: in a later play, Cleopatra will address similar

lines to the wretchedly victorious Octavius. Brutus recognizes here the necessary end of "his life's history": all, from the very start, has tended to this gesture. In it we may find, as in Hamlet's death, "the vision of life in its entirety, the sense of fulfillment that lifts [the hero] above his defeat." Brutus's death is the action which resolves the phantasmal "interim" and ends the "insurrection" in "the state of man."

And this gesture receives, as the assassination of Caesar did not, the requisite assent. Brutus "hath honour by his death," says Strato; and Lucilius, "So Brutus should be found." The opposing parties join together now in Octavius's service, and it is Antony himself who can pronounce the epitaph, "This was the noblest Roman of them all." His words and the gestures are universally accepted.

But what of Rome and its future? I said [elsewhere] that the esthetic satisfaction of the perfected tragic form is a "truth" to be accepted only provisionally—and it is the close involvement of *Julius Caesar* with widely known historical facts which forces upon us the recognition of that truth's limitations. Indeed, the play contains hints—the bloody, divisive course of the triumvirate has been made plain, for instance—which, even without prior historical knowledge, might make us temper our optimism over the play's conclusion. With Brutus's death the play has revealed its tragic entelechy; the destined shape has been found, and the discovery brings its esthetic satisfactions. That the price of our pleasure is the hero's death is not (as in *King Lear* it will so terribly be) a source of discomfort. But what we cannot dismiss is our knowledge that every end is also a beginning. History will have its way; "fate" will defeat men's "wills"; and the "glory" of this "losing day" will tarnish and become, in the movement of time, as ambiguous as the glorious loss on the ides of March.

Thus we must entertain two apparently opposite points of view. With Brutus's sacrificial gesture the ritual has been found which can satisfy the dramatic expectations created by the play. The final words are spoken, the language is understood; and thus the play has given us what Robert Frost demanded of all poetry, "a momentary stay against confusion." But if we stress in Frost's definition his modifying word *momentary*, we find ourselves cast back upon history; and once out of the timeless world of the play, "confusion" predominates. Shakespeare, I believe, recognized this.

Dream and Interpretation:
Julius Caesar

Marjorie B. Garber

In the final act of *Julius Caesar*, Cassius, fearful of defeat at Philippi, dispatches Titinius to discover whether the surrounding troops are friends or enemies. He posts another soldier to observe, and when the soldier sees Titinius encircled by horsemen and reports that he is taken, Cassius runs on his sword and dies. Shortly afterward, Titinius reenters the scene bearing a "wreath of victory" from Brutus. When he sees the dead body, he at once understands Cassius's tragic mistake. "Alas, thou has misconstrued everything!" (5.3.84), he cries out, and he too runs on Cassius's sword.

That one cry, "thou hast misconstrued everything!" might well serve as an epigraph for the whole of *Julius Caesar*. The play is full of omens and portents, augury and dream, and almost without exception these omens are misinterpreted. Calpurnia's dream, the dream of Cinna the poet, the advice of the augurers, all suggest one course of action and produce its opposite. The compelling dream imagery of the play, which should, had it been rightly interpreted, have persuaded Caesar to avoid the Capitol and Cinna not to go forth, is deflected by the characters of men, making tragedy inevitable. For *Julius Caesar* is not only a political play, but also a play of character. Its imagery of dream and sign, an imagery so powerful that it enters the plot on the level of action, is a means of examining character and consciousness.

From *Dream in Shakespeare: From Metaphor to Metamorphosis*. © 1974 by Yale University. Yale University Press, 1974.

Much of the plot of *Julius Caesar*, like that of *Richard III*, is shaped by the device of the predictive dream or sign. The two plays also have another point of similarity, not unrelated to the device of dream: each divides men into two camps, those who attempt to control dream and destiny and those who are controlled by it. In *Richard III* only Gloucester thinks himself able to master dream and turn it to his own purposes; Edward, Clarence, and Hastings are its helpless victims. *Julius Caesar*, on the other hand, presents a number of characters who declare themselves indifferent to dream or contemptuous of its power: Cassius, who so firmly places the fault not in our stars but in ourselves; Decius Brutus, who deliberately misinterprets Calpurnia's prophetic dream to serve his own ends; Octavius, in whom the whole dimension of emotion seems lacking; and Caesar himself. Caesar's conviction, however, is notably wavering as the play begins. As Cassius points out to the conspirators,

> he is superstitious grown of late,
> Quite from the main opinion he held once
> Of fantasy, of dreams, and ceremonies.
>
> (2.1.195–97)

Caesar struggles against this tendency, repeatedly invoking his public persona to quell his private fears: "Danger knows full well," he boasts, "That Caesar is more dangerous than he" (2.2.44–45). Yet he protests too much.

In his susceptibility to dream and introspection he stands midway between the coldness of Decius Brutus and the blind self-preoccupation of Brutus. For Brutus is in a way the least self-aware of all these characters, because he thinks of himself as a supremely rational man. Again and again he confronts his situation and misinterprets it, secure in his own erroneous sense of self. His frequent solitary ruminations have a certain poignancy about them; they approach a truth and reject it through lack of self-knowledge. Thus he meditates,

> Between the acting of a dreadful thing
> And the first motion, all the interim is
> Like a phantasma, or a hideous dream:
> The genius and the mortal instruments
> Are then in council; and the state of man,
> Like to a little kingdom, suffers then
> The nature of an insurrection.
>
> (2.1.63–69)

Yet in the next moment he turns his back on this foreboding and welcomes the conspirators to his house. It is Brutus who sees the ghost of Caesar and is indifferent to him; Brutus who is afflicted with a revealing insomnia: "Since Cassius first did whet me against Caesar," he says, "I have not slept" (2.1.61–62). Like Gloucester, Macbeth, and Henry IV, all similarly blind to self, he bears his crime on his conscience and cannot sleep, though he is visited by an apparition which seems to come from the dream state. There is a poignant moment after the ghost's first appearance, when he tries in vain to convince his servants and soldiers that they have cried out in the night:

> BRUTUS: Didst thou dream, Lucius, that thou so criedst
>   out?
> LUCIUS: My lord, I do not know that I did cry.
> BRUTUS: Yes, that thou didst. Didst thou see anything?
> LUCIUS: Nothing, my lord.
> BRUTUS: Sleep again, Lucius. Sirrah Claudius!
>   (*To Varro*). Fellow thou, awake!
> VARRO: My lord?
> CLAUDIUS: My lord?
> BRUTUS: Why did you so cry out, sirs, in your sleep?
> BOTH: Did we, my lord?
> BRUTUS: Ay. Saw you anything?
> VARRO: No, my lord, I saw nothing.
> CLAUDIUS: Nor I, my lord.
>   (4.3.291–301)

Nowhere is the quintessential loneliness of the conscience-stricken man more forcefully portrayed. "Nothing, my lord." Brutus, too, has misconstrued everything, and his tragedy is that he suspects it. Trapped by his high-minded vanity and his inability to function in the world of action—trapped, that is, by his own character—he sees the Rome he tried to rescue in ruins as a result of his act.

Caesar's ghost appears to Brutus in the source for *Julius Caesar*, Plutarch's *Lives of the Noble Grecians and Romans*. Its presence is also related to the Senecan theatrical tradition we have discussed above. Psychologically, it can be seen as an extension of Brutus's guilt feelings; like Richard III's Bosworth dream or the appearance of Banquo's ghost, the apparition here presents itself to one man only and is not sensed by the others present. Such visionary dream figures are found in Shakespeare only in plays which are directly concerned with the psychological condition of the characters; the disappearance of the ghost as a type in the plays following *Macbeth* is a sign, not merely of dramaturgical sophistication, but also of a shift in emphasis. For *Julius Caesar* is, in a way, the last play of its kind. The uses of dream, vision, and omen will change sharply in the plays that follow.

The motif of the misinterpreted dream in this play becomes a main factor in the dramatic action, demonstrating, always, some crucial fact about the interpreter. In the second scene of the play the soothsayer's warning goes unheeded, though in the same scene Caesar betrays his superstitious cast of mind. The contrast is adeptly managed: Antony is reminded to touch Calpurnia in the course of his race on the Lupercal, to remove her "sterile curse" (1.2.9). But when the soothsayer cautions Caesar to "beware the ides of March" (l. 18), he rejects the intended warning out of hand;

> He is a dreamer, let us leave him. Pass.
>
> (1.2.24)

The inference is that dreams, like omens, are of no value; "dreamer" is a pejorative dismissal, akin to "madman." Calpurnia may have need of supernatural aid, but not the public Caesar. Already in this early scene we see him assuming a position closer to that of gods than men, a thoughtless hubris which is in itself dangerous. The omen, intrinsically a kind of dramatic device, is chiefly significant because it indicates his lack of self-knowledge.

The next scene, like much of the play, is in part at least a landscape of the mind. Casca, who is to be one of the conspirators, apprehensively reports to Cicero the strange events of the day. The heavens are "dropping fire" (1.3.10), a slave's hand flames but does not burn, a lion walks in the Capitol, an owl sits in the marketplace at noon. These omens are all reported by Plutarch, but Shakespeare turns them to dramatic purpose, making them mirror the conspirators' mood. "When these prodigies / Do so conjointly meet," says Casca,

> let not men say,
> "These are their reasons, they are natural,"
> For I believe they are portentous things
> Unto the climate that they point upon.
>
> (1.3.28–32)

To this superstitious view Cicero has a wise and moderate reply.

> Indeed, it is a strange-disposèd time:
> But men may construe things after their fashion,
> Clean from the purpose of the things themselves.
>
> (ll. 33–35)

This is Titinius's lament: "Thou hast misconstrued everything." Like all the quasi-oracular pronouncements in this play, it is two-edged. Men may construe things as they like for their own purposes; just so Cassius plays on Brutus's fears of monarchy to enlist his help. And men may also misconstrue through error; so Caesar misreads the signs which might have kept him from death. But if Cicero's answer is apposite, it is also bloodless and dispassionate. What he does not consider is the element of humanity, the energy of men's passions inflamed by supposed signs. He is outside the tragedy, a choric figure who does not reenter the drama.

More and more it becomes evident that signs and dreams are morally neutral elements, incapable of effect without interpretation. By structuring his play around them, Shakespeare invites us to scrutinize the men who read the signs—to witness the tragedy of misconstruction. The two senses of Cicero's maxim, the willful deceiver and the willingly deceived, are the controllers of dream and the controlled. Decius Brutus, perhaps the coldest in a play replete with cold men, states the position of the former unequivocally. No matter how superstitious Caesar has lately become, he, Decius Brutus, is confident of his ability to manipulate him.

> I can o'ersway him; for he loves to hear
> That unicorns may be betrayed with trees,
> And bears with glasses, elephants with holes,
> Lions with toils, and men with flatterers;
> But when I tell him he hates flatterers,
> He says he does, being then most flattered.
> Let me work;
> For I can give his humor the true bent,
> And I will bring him to the Capitol.
>
> (2.1.203–11)

Willful misconstruction is his purpose and his art. And, fulfilling his promise, it is Decius Brutus who artfully misinterprets Calpurnia's dream and coaxes Caesar to the scene of his death.

Calpurnia's dream is one of the play's cruxes. By this time in the course of the drama an internal convention has been established regarding dreams and omens: whatever their source, they are true, and it is dangerous to disregard them. Shakespeare's audience would certainly have been familiar with the story of Julius Caesar, and such a collection of portents and premonitions would have seemed to them, as it does to us, to be infallibly leading to the moment of murder. Calpurnia herself adds to the catalogue of unnatural events:

> A lioness hath whelped in the streets,
> And graves have yawned, and yielded up their dead;
> Fierce fiery warriors fought upon the clouds
> In ranks and squadrons and right form of war,
> Which drizzled blood upon the Capitol;
> The noise of battle hurtled in the air,
> Horses did neigh and dying men did groan,
> And ghosts did shriek and squeal about the streets.
>
> (2.2.17–24)

This is in fact an apocalypse of sorts, the last judgment of Rome. Unlike the events narrated by Casca, those reported by Calpurnia are not specified in Plutarch; it is noteworthy how much more *Shakespearean* they are, and how economically chosen to foreshadow, metaphorically, the later events of the play. The lioness is Wrath, and from her loins will spring forth "ranks and squadrons and right form of war," while the ghost of Caesar appears solemnly in the streets. Shakespeare was to remember this moment soon again, upon the appearance of the most majestic of all his ghosts.

> In the most high and palmy state of Rome,
> A little ere the mightiest Julius fell,
> The graves stood tenantless, and the sheeted dead
> Did squeak and gibber in the Roman streets.
>
> (*Hamlet* 1.1.113–16)

Calpurnia's bona fides as a prophetess is thus firmly established by the time we hear her dream, and so too is the blind obstinacy of Caesar. He willfully misinterprets a message from his augurers, who advise him to stay away from the Capitol, alarmed by the sacrifice of a beast in which they found no heart. "Caesar should be a beast without a heart," he declares, "If he should stay at home today for fear" (2.2.42–43), thus completely reversing the message of the haruspices. In this mood he is interrupted by Decius Brutus, whose wiliness outlasts his own more heedless cunning. Caesar is one of those elder statesmen who visibly enjoys causing discomfort to his underlings; it is partially for this reason that he now abruptly changes his mind upon the entrance of Decius and declares "I will not come" (l. 71). We have not yet heard the dream; Shakespeare leaves it for Caesar himself to recount, as he does now to Decius.

> She dreamt tonight she saw my statue,
> Which, like a fountain with an hundred spouts,
> Did run pure blood, and many lusty Romans
> Came smiling and did bathe their hands in it.
> And these does she apply for warnings and portents
> And evils imminent, and on her knee
> Hath begged that I will stay at home today.
>
> (2.2.76–82)

We may notice that here, as in our interpretation of Romeo's last dream [elsewhere], the dead man becomes a statue; this is a recurrent conceit in Shakespearean dreams, and in *The Winter's Tale,* as we will see, the dream action becomes plot as Hermione "dies," becomes a "statue," and is reborn. In Calpurnia's dream the latent dream thoughts are not far removed from the manifest content. She interprets the statue as the body of Caesar and also his funerary monument, and the gushing forth of blood she reads as death. As a prophetic dream this is both an accurate and a curiously lyrical one, graceful in its imagery. It forecasts directly the assassination before the Capitol.

Decius, however, is prepared for the event, and he begins immediately to discredit Calpurnia's prediction. He commences with what is by now a familiar note: "This dream is all amiss interpreted," and offers instead his own "interpretation":

> It was a vision fair and fortunate:
> Your statue spouting blood in many pipes,
> In which so many smiling Romans bathed,
> Signifies that from you great Rome shall suck
> Reviving blood, and that great men shall press
> For tinctures, stains, relics and cognizance.
> This by Calpurnia's dream is signified.
>
> (ll. 83–90)

It is the dissimulator now who cries, "thou hast misconstrued everything." He takes the manifest content of Calpurnia's dream and attributes to it a clever if wholly fabricated set of latent thoughts, which are the more impressive for their psychological insight. Caesar is flattered, as Decius had predicted, and resolves to go to the Capitol. His last doubts are abruptly erased when Decius suggests that he will be offered a crown and warns that refusal to go will seem like uxoriousness:

> it were a mock
> Apt to be rendered, for someone to say
> "Break up the Senate till another time,
> When Caesar's wife shall meet with better dreams."
> (2.2.96–99)

This is a thrust well calculated to strike home. But there is a curious ambiguity about Calpurnia's dream, and the real irony of the situation is that Decius's spurious interpretation of it is as true in its way as Calpurnia's.

The content of her dream, it may be pointed out, does not itself appear in Plutarch. "She dreamed," he writes, "that Caesar was slain, and that she had him in her arms," and he also tells us that "Titus Livius writeth, that it was in this sort. The Senate having set upon the top of Caesar's house, for an ornament and setting forth of the same, a certain pinnacle, Calpurnia dreamed that she saw it broken down." But the dream as we have it, the spouting statue and the smiling Romans, is a Shakespearean interpolation. Like Romeo's last dream, which we have already examined [elsewhere], it is chiefly remarkable for the fact that it permits two opposite interpretations, the one literal and the other metaphorical. For Decius's flattery,

> that from you great Rome shall suck
> Reviving blood, and that great men shall press
> For tinctures, stains, relics, and cognizance

is also a truth. Antony's funeral oration turns on precisely this point, elevating the slain Caesar to the status of a saint or a demigod, exhibiting the bloody wounds to win the hearts of the crowd. And at the play's end Antony shares hegemony—however uneasily—with the *novus homo* Octavius, literal descendant of Caesar's "blood."

The presence of Calpurnia's dream at this crucial point in the plot is thus trebly determined: (1) it has Plutarchan authority and is thus an original element in the story; (2) it acts as a functional device to further the action, showing the deliberate blindness of Caesar to a warning which would have saved his life and demonstrating the cold-blooded manipulation of the conspirators; (3) it symbolically foreshadows events to come, supporting the theme of "all amiss interpreted" which is central to the play's meaning. Interestingly, the accustomed tension between the men who aspire to control dream and those who are controlled by it is diminished in this episode; Decius, who means to assert control, is in a larger sense controlled, since he does not see that his interpretation is true.

For all its richness, however, the scene of Calpurnia's dream is rivaled in significance by a much more tangential scene, which seems at first glance oddly out of place in the plot. The scene of Cinna the poet is in many ways the most symbolically instructive of the whole play: it demonstrates in action the same theme of misinterpretation with which we have been so much concerned. Cinna the poet, a character unrelated to his namesake Cinna the conspirator, appears only in this scene, which may be seen as a kind of emblem for the entire meaning of *Julius Caesar*. We encounter him as he makes his way along a Roman street, and his opening lines describe his dream.

> I dreamt tonight that I did feast with Caesar,
> And things unluckily charge my fantasy.
> I have no will to wander forth of doors,
> Yet something leads me forth.
>
> (3.3.1–4)

To "feast with Caesar" here means to share his fate—we may remember Brutus's "Let's carve him as a dish fit for the gods" (2.1.173). Cinna admits that he has had a premonition of danger, but that he has chosen to disregard it; "something"—misconstruction again—leads him forth. He is set on by a group of plebians, their emotions raised to fever pitch by Antony's oration, and they rapidly catechize him on his identity and purpose.

> THIRD PLEBIAN: Your name sir, truly.
> CINNA: Truly, my name is Cinna.
> FIRST PLEBIAN: Tear him to pieces! He's a conspirator.
> CINNA: I am Cinna the poet! I am Cinna the poet!
> FOURTH PLEBIAN: Tear him for his bad verses! Tear him for
>   his bad verses!
> CINNA: I am not Cinna the conspirator.

FOURTH PLEBIAN: It is no matter, his name's Cinna; pluck
but his name out of his heart, and turn him going.
(3.3.27–34)

The scene is a perfect illustration of Cicero's verdict: "Men may
construe things after their fashion, / Clean from the purpose of the
things themselves." The taking of the name for the man—a the-
matically important element throughout this play, where Caesar is
at once a private man and a public title—is symbolic of the overt
confusion manifest in much of the action. Cinna's dream is a legit-
imate cause for anxiety, which he chooses to ignore at peril to himself.
Plutarch supplied him with a practical motive: "When he heard that
they carried Caesar's body to burial, being ashamed not to accom-
pany his funerals: he went out of his house"; in Shakespeare's version
the cause is deliberately less exact, more psychological than circum-
stantial. The warning is given and ignored; the plebians do not care
that they attack the wrong man. In one short scene of less than forty
lines the whole myth of the play is concisely expressed.

Julius Caesar is a complex and ambiguous play, which does not
concern itself principally with political theory, but rather with the
strange blindness of the rational mind—in politics and elsewhere—
to the great irrational powers which flow through life and control
it. The significance attached to the theme of "thou hast misconstrued
everything" clearly depends to a large extent upon the reading—or
misreading—of the play's many dreams. Here, in the last of his plays
to use dreams and omens primarily as devices of plot, Shakespeare
again demonstrates the great symbolic power which resides in the
dream, together with its remarkable capacity for elucidating aspects
of the play which otherwise remain in shadow.

*J*ulius *Caesar:* Social Order
and the Kinetic World

Michael Long

We have, . . . two ways of approaching the basic thought-model which shapes and contains Shakespeare's tragic vision. We may move in the direction of realism from the symbolic Law/Nature conflict of the festive comedies; or we may move in the direction of social variety and specific detail from the archetypal tragic theories of Nietzsche and Schopenhauer. The two converge on the vision of the plays of the great tragic period, upon which it is now time to embark. And at the entrance to that period there stands the tragic story of a single man, Brutus in *Julius Caesar*.

The play in which the tragedy of Brutus is to be found is neither so great nor so coherent a work as the others which I shall analyse [elsewhere]. It is, I think, essentially exploratory and tentative, its shifts in focus and tone being an index of the extreme caution with which Shakespeare handles the issues involved in the play. It does not present Rome, and the social psychology of Rome, with the same comprehensiveness and coherence as *Coriolanus* and *Antony and Cleopatra*. And its hesitation about the value of Caesarism does not suggest to me any deliberate and resolved ambivalence—rather a decision to beg the question and to bide time. It lacks a dramatically functioning network of structuring images, which suggests that the thought from which it derives does not involve the coherence of vision and depth-analysis to which such imagery in Shakespeare normally bears witness. Unlike *Troilus and Cressida* and *Measure for*

From *The Unnatural Scene*. © 1976 by Michael Long. Methuen, 1976.

Measure it is a real "problem play," dichotomous and contradictory in itself where they are only problematic in that they present critics with tones and analyses which they find hard to stomach.

But the tragedy of Brutus which lies within the play is coherent enough; coherent enough indeed to suggest, as we contemplate it, aspects of the whole Shakespearean vision to which it is an introduction. It overwhelms the play in which it is set, for it is on the figure of Brutus that Shakespeare's mature tragic imagination settled, and it is in him that we can first examine what that imagination produces as it contemplates the limiting qualities of human cultures and codes.

Brutus is an extremely civilized man. If we think in terms of moral probity, scruple, courage, selflessness, good-humour in the face of adversity, honesty, incorruptibility, tenderness and kindness, courtesy and politeness—if we think in terms of these criteria, which must stand high on any ethical scale, then Brutus comes out as an extremely virtuous man. And the virtuousness, having everything to do with what it is to be civilized and socialized, consists in a readiness to use the powers of his mind to calculate maximum benefit for others and thereby to make morally responsible judgements. And what this virtuous, civilized, quiet-voiced, sober, intelligent and painstaking man achieves is utter desolation. He murders his friend; he brings about mob violence and civil war leading eventually to the disenchanted suicides of himself and another friend; and he shatters his domestic peace (which is finely registered in the play) to such a degree that his erstwhile tranquil and devoted wife runs distracted and kills herself in a particularly hideous fashion, by swallowing hot coals. Nemesis was never a more dismally ironic force. No other Shakespearean tragic protagonist is quite so unimpeachable as Brutus; but none is the creator of any more complete futility and desolation. One can almost hear Schopenhauer's acidic recognition of the kind of tale it is.

A bleak, tragic irony, then, about one way of being "civilized" or "virtuous"; and a tragic irony which will take us well into the whole vision of the tragic plays. As we describe Brutus as "civilized," "cultivated," "intelligent" or "scrupulous" we do so in a way which makes us aware of the radical limitations, as well as qualities, to which those words point. The words of praise begin to suggest debilitating circumscriptions, having principally to do with a loss of responsive and perceptive powers. When we say that Brutus brings his intelligence to bear on problems of moral judgment we begin to realize that we are saying that that is *all* that he brings. He does not bring to bear an entire and experiencing "self" or "sensibility" so much as an intricate, ratiocinative instrument working within the necessarily selective and hence reductive terms of his particular codes. He works with Nietzsche's Socratic assumption that the universe is knowable and, being known, corrigible; and with that kind of language which Schopenhauer would call "conceptual" as opposed to "perceptive," too high up in the "edifice of reflection" to do anything except grossly distort. And he frames his moral thinking within terms of the best ethical systems that he has learnt—principally stoicism—and thus lives a moral life which is representative in an exemplary way of the inherited, shared and acknowledged wisdom gathered within those systems.

The result is that he experiences himself and others in a peculiarly debilitated way. The debilitation stems from overcodification, and that in its turn from his being so civilized, so utterly a social being. His opening confession in the play (though he of course does not realize what a major confession of human weakness it is) registers this debilitation very strongly:

> I am not gamesome: I do lack some part
> Of that quick spirit that is in Antony.
>
> (1.2.28–29)

What Brutus appears to have said, and doubtless thinks he has said, is that he is not such a wassailer as Antony; but in the light of what I have said about kinesis and festive release [elsewhere] the simple word "gamesome" takes on a bigger, and sadder, aspect. It begins to suggest an isolation from kinds of generative, organic power without which life is sterile—something which goes far towards explaining that lifeless indifference which gradually enshrouds the oddly passive figure of Brutus as his tragedy progresses.

This sense of an isolation from the generative powers of the kinetic recurs in many ways throughout the play. It is arguable that Cassius, who knows him well, is permitting himself an irony of some shrewdness when, after Brutus has listened politely to his complaints against Caesar and promised to consider the matter in good time, he confesses himself

> glad that my weak words
> Have struck but thus much show of fire from Brutus,
>
> (1.2.176–77)

for there is something terribly and poignantly accurate about the ironic possibilities of the word "show." Certainly, insofar as it suggests the absence of any real inflammabilities in the personality of Brutus it touches a key theme of the play; and one which, for example, will be in our minds again when we see how, at the murder itself, Brutus is lacking in that kind of deep and spontaneous emotional conviction which "fire" suggests. When he bids his fellow conspirators to

> let our hearts, as subtle masters do,
> Stir up their servants to an act of rage,
> And after seem to chide 'em
>
> (2.1.175–77)

he is talking as a man in whom the immediate instigation of the emotive is absent and who therefore must have recourse to a false and substitute version of it, induced into action, to give him the necessary generative prompting.

The "clinical," "abstract" and overcodified qualities of Brutus's sensibility, then, are functions of his alienation from the generative and instigatory powers of the kinetic. He is not "gamesome"; and that, in the context of Shakespeare's tragic metaphysic, is quite enough to make all his virtues and all his civilized scruples balefully inadequate. As we follow the dismal course of his life it is this distance from basic energies which comes through again and again. Indeed it is a distance which we see him sedulous to preserve, as he quite deliberately buries his innermost psychic movements so that their energies go continuously untapped and their promptings continuously ignored. Thus his attitude to the "phantasma" or "hideous dream" which comes "between the acting of a dreadful thing / And the first motion" is simply that it must be ridden out like a storm. It is a temporary disorder of entirely negative significance, an "insurrection"—like the "figures" and "fantasies / Which busy care draws in the brains of men." They are all the insignificant figments of wayward imagination which occasionally disrupt the measured calm of the civilized mind and which Brutus tends to attribute to simple physical causes, like "tiredness" or (with Caesar's ghost) "the weakness of mine eyes." The inner energies of the psyche are for him what they were for Theseus—airy nothings of interest only to poets who, for some reason, are curiously given to rolling their eyes in a fine frenzy. Brutus (who, one remembers, thinks that poets are "jigging fools") can never contemplate the possibility that the play of such energies is in any way essential to the business of being human. When they present themselves troublesomely in his mind so that "poor Brutus (is) with himself at war," his reaction is to close himself about them and withhold them from expression or communication. In this condition the mind is only an interim and untidy version of its civilized self, something which cannot be of interest even to his friends. These "passions of some difference" breed "conceptions only proper to myself."

One might say, with an eye to Nietzsche's terms, that the military encampment of Apollo in his mind is ruinously complete, its order-idea become "pathological . . . imposing itself on us as crass reality." Or alternatively, looking back to the festive-comic model in its handling of such things, one might say that he lacks Holofernes' "good gift" whereby the apprehensions of an extravagant spirit are begot, nourished and delivered in an alive and breeding mind. Just as we come from *Love's Labour's Lost* with an idea of the healthy mind as a chaos of swarming fertility whose offspring hunger for deliverance, and with a sense that there is something inalienably mirthful in this process of unimpeded creativity, so we come from the humourless Brutus with a sense of this creativity held down and suppressed by a man who is determined to be calm, resolute and contained. The most powerful and terrible image of this is that in which he counsels Cassius to bottle up the anger he feels in the quarrel scene at Sardis—to force its energies back within "though it do split you." This fearsome readiness to hold in the energies of the psyche under damaging pressure, in the name of an idea of what constitutes the "civilized," is the basis of Brutus's attitude to the kinetic. And it is also the key to his tragic sterility.

This stance—fatally impervious to the kinetic, and so successful in resisting its intrusions into his calm social bearing that, as Plutarch had said, he was able to

frame and fashion his countenance and looks that no man
could discern he had anything to trouble his mind—

is enough to be the cause of the desolation, sterility and ennui which is Brutus's life. All his "even virtue," "untired spirits" and "formal constancy"; all that Roman courage which "will not falter" and which will urge others to "be not affrighted"; all the "kind love, good thoughts, and reverence" of a spirit "full of good regards" and "armed so strong in honesty"—all these come to their dismal parody of a fruition in his ending "sick of many griefs" as a natural consequence of his being a *merely* civilized man in a Shakespearean universe. It is the same lack which makes him so fatally ignorant of what fluid human contact is—the ignorance which makes him "stubborn" and "strange" in friendship, and which makes him pathetically confident that he will win the friendship of Antony by appealing rationally and calmly to a bundle of mere *values*.

The result, as I have said, is sterility and ennui; but there is something particularly baleful in this ennui of the civilized mind and something especially painful in the way in which we see him experience it. We can appreciate this if we compare him for a moment, as he has been usefully compared before, with Macbeth; for Macbeth is also driven back to a condition of torpor and resigned defeat which stems from his having cut himself off from the nourishing and life-giving powers of the world. But Macbeth is man enough, or animal enough, to know what he has lost, to know the pleasures of the creatural world which are now denied him, and to be ready to fight like a bear to retain life. But there is something far more destitute than this in Brutus, for he is so civilized, so trained in readiness to accept the curtailment and, if necessary, the elimination of creatural life in the name of a social cause ("when it shall please my country to need my death") that he cannot even recognize, let alone protest against, the abysmal dwindling of life in himself when it comes.

Thus, when he has permitted himself the momentary confession that he is sick of many griefs, he immediately gathers himself again, on being reminded of his "philosophy," into that determination which is represented by the claim that "no man bears sorrow better." From here on he will "endure with patience" and without protest. But this, which for him represents a noble forbearance in the face of the world's trials, is felt by us as a painful exhibition of moral irrelevance almost to the point of the outrageous. He buries all creatural protest against the news of his wife's death, fortified by reliance on his stoic exercises of meditation, just as, when he faces death himself, "he meditates" himself into the required mood of indifference. His version of Macbeth's "tomorrow and tomorrow and tomorrow" is characteristically without complaint. His expectations of fulfilment have been drastically reduced by his moral cogitations:

> That we shall die, we know; 'tis but the time,
> And drawing days out, that men stand upon;
>
> (3.1.100–101)

so that now, as the days begin to draw out, he is ready to be satisfied with the bleak comforts of his knowledge—"it sufficeth that the day will end," "I know my hour will come." Trained in a civilized ethic which is hostile to so many aspects of Shakespearean kinesis—to the imagination, to creatural need, to instinctive quickness of sympathy—he is ready simply to bow his head before adversity and accept with meekness the destruction of himself by forces which he has disabled himself from understanding or even apprehending. His decline is eventually into an unimpassioned and unprotesting grief which simply inundates his being and reduces him to silence:

> Now is that noble vessel full of grief,
> That it runs over even at his eyes.
>
> (5.5.13–14)

The last twist of the knife is given at the end of the play. It is bitterly appropriate that the members of his society who survive him should deem it fit to exalt his nobility and see to it that his funeral be "ordered honourably," for the way in which they laud and revere his memory—in Roman civic terms of honour, nobility, honesty, sense of the common good, virtue, order and purity of motive— grates on our ears with tragic irony as it is announced by Antony and Octavius. The things which serve in the Roman mind to redeem him from being a mere conspirator are for us the very things which made his life so bleak. As will later be the case with other tragedies in which a civic code proves itself so inadequate to life, nobody has learned anything. A society will go on unchanged. With Shakespeare one cannot be so sure as one can with Milton that there will be a new acquist of true experience from a great tragic event. He never underestimates the imperviousness of social man to the experience of tragedy, and the difficulty which social man will have in accommodating himself to the traumatic critique of his values and attachments which tragedy makes.

Plutarch said of Brutus that,

> having framed his manners of life by the rules of virtue
> and study of philosophy, and having employed his wit,

> which was gentle and constant, in attempting of great things, methinks he was rightly made and framed unto virtue.

The words which North used in his translation—"framed," "rules," "employed his wit," "constant"—must have provided the mind which had created the kinetic world of the festive comedies with food for ironic thought; and what came out of that thought is the dismal tragedy of the dramatic protagonist's life. The underview of Brutus's civilized values which results is more than the traditional Christian critique of the Stoic as lacking "love." The criticism is total, not local. It is not a matter of one missing feature, but of something lacking in the entire grain of the man. What Brutus lacks is something far greater, far more energetic, but also far more commonplace than what is ordinarily meant by Christians when they talk of "love." It is nature's volatility, everything that is touched on by that single word "gamesome," everything that the festive comedies have made of "nature"—quickness, passion, impulse, wit, equivocation, laughter, forgetfulness, irresponsibility. It is the Mercutio element that is lacking: it is Brutus's tragedy that he would have thought Queen Mab was the passing affliction of a care-worn mind.

Nearer to the essence of Shakespeare's view of this civilized Stoic is that of Schopenhauer:

> The Stoic sage as represented by this ethical system, could never obtain life or inner poetical truth, but remains a wooden, stiff lay-figure with whom one can do nothing. He himself does not know where to go with his wisdom, and his perfect peace, contentment, and blessedness directly contradict the nature of mankind.

Though the Christian critique of Stoicism must have contributed considerably to Shakespeare's sense of Brutus's tragic shortcomings, his final viewpoint is different. Schopenhauer is nearer to it, because he, with his remarkably energetic conception of the kinetic world of *die Wille*, thinks within terms of some of the same polarities as does Shakespeare.

"Thou Bleeding Piece of Earth": The Ritual Ground of *Julius Caesar*

Naomi Conn Liebler

Shakespeare's *Julius Caesar* begins at the Feast of the Lupercal, the Roman celebration which took place on February 13–15 and which, in the play, quickly passes into history's most famous ides of March. Among those readers who attach any significance at all to this opening, Shakespeare's conflation of the festival and Caesar's assassination is understood primarily as a "dramatic economy," a structural device for the exposition of the main characters and the juxtaposition of the rather "sporty" aspects of the holiday to the more serious political business of conspiracy, murder, and civil war to follow. Usually the critical focus is upon act 1, scene 2, which reveals Caesar's superstitious nature (as he urges Calphurnia to stand in Antony's way when he runs in the "holy chase") and contrasts Antony with Brutus: the latter is "not gamesome" and lacks "some part / Of that quick spirit that is in Antony" (ll. 28–29).

Certainly exposition of character and atmosphere is a conventional and important purpose of opening scenes in any Shakespearean play, and "so let it be with *Caesar*." But while contrasting characters and atmospheres are being established here, something else is going on: the Lupercal is a *specific* kind of holiday having ritual and political importance, and thus it is especially appropriate as the opening of *Julius Caesar*. As Rome's most ancient festival of purgation and fertility, it provides more than a vague ceremonial background for the

From *Shakespeare Studies* 14 (1981). © 1981 by the Council for Research in the Renaissance.

play. It sets a specific context for Brutus's "ritual" idea of the assassination and the failure of his design, and the ground against which the political and religious changes in Rome can be seen in relief.

For most of the play's characters, as much as for its later critics, the Lupercal seems to be no more than a minor distraction. Indeed, if Shakespeare had omitted all reference to the holiday, he could have begun the play with Cassius's approach to Brutus, and avoided the conflation of a month's time. That he did not do so must therefore call our attention to the holiday itself, first of all to learn what he knew about it, and then to explore how its inclusion might affect our reading of the play. I am going to suggest in this essay that Shakespeare knew more about the practice and significance of the Lupercalian rites than is given in the traditionally accepted sources for the play, North's translation of Plutarch's *Lives* of Caesar, Antony, and Brutus; that his knowledge came from a fourth and equally accessible source; that he referred to the Lupercalia in this play as a ritual violated rather than observed; and that since he himself was part of a society steeped in social, political, and religious rituals of its own, he might well have used the Lupercalia as a device to show the implicit dangers to the common weal of ignoring or contravening such rituals.

In a way, we have *had* to ignore the specific nature of the Lupercalian rites because, although ample information about them is available to us (in Ovid's *Fasti,* for instance), it has not been clear that this lore was available to Shakespeare. The three Plutarchan *Lives* in fact provide very little information about the festival, and we have had to assume that this was all Shakespeare could have known about it. The references to the Lupercal in the *Lives* of Caesar and Antony (there are none in that of Brutus) are playful: in the *Life of Caesar* we learn only that it was "the feast of sheap heards or heard men," that the race was run by "divers noble mens sonnes . . . striking in sport them they meete in their way with leather thonges . . . to make them geve place," and that some women believed that receiving these blows would cure barrenness and ease childbirth. Similarly, in the *Life of Antony* we read again of the "sport of the runners," who, "running naked up and downe the city . . . for pleasure do strike them they meete in their way." Descriptions of the Lupercalia in Shakespeare's other known sources—Appian, Livy, Ovid's *Metamorphoses*—are negligible. The material he might have read in Cooper's popular *Thesaurus Linguae Romanae & Britannicae* (printed five times between 1565 and 1587), in Elyot's *Dictionary*, or in Charles Stephanus's Latin *Thesaurus*, is brief and adds little to what can be found in the *Life of Caesar*. There is a good deal of interesting but secondary lore in Stephen Batman's 1577 *Golden Book of the Leaden Gods*, but to seek there Shakespeare would have needed to know with which "Leaden God" to associate the Lupercalia.

In fact, Shakespeare did not have to look in any dictionary or read any Latin in order to learn all he needed to know about the festival (and nearly as much as the *Fasti* would have provided). His source had been before him from his first encounter with North's Plutarch, for there, in the *Life of Romulus* (the first Roman *Life* in the collection), is a substantive account of the festival, its history and implications, and some hint of its actual as well as its metaphoric relation to the last days of Julius Caesar. For example, the *Romulus* reveals that the Lupercalia were rites of purgation and fertility whose precise origins were lost to history; that they were associated with the figure of Romulus and therefore with the foundation of Roman civilization; that Caesar himself was involved in their observation and preservation; and that much of what Plutarch was later to say about the rise and fall of Caesar he had already said about that of Romulus. The careers of the two bear some remarkable resemblances which would not have escaped Shakespeare's notice, since the civilization that so powerfully captured his imagination began with the one and effectively ended with the other.

A reading of the *Romulus* offers us more than just another item for source-study. It suggests, first of all, why the play begins at the Lupercalia: this opening sets in our minds the context of an ancient religious festival overshadowed and swallowed up by the more modern pragmatic and secular concerns of politics, which are generally accepted as the primary interests of the play. The first scene creates a sense that something is rotting—if not rotten—in the "high and palmy state" of Rome. The occasion is indeed a holiday, but there is some confusion about just what is being celebrated. For the carpenter and cobbler, the cause is Caesar's victory "over Pompey's blood"; for the tribune Marullus, the celebration of that victory is a sacrilege: "Run to your houses, fall upon your knees, / Pray to the gods to intermit the plague / That needs must light on this ingratitude" (ll. 53–55). It is Marullus who remembers that the day is the Feast of the Lupercal (l. 67), and tries to maintain its age-old sanctity. The conflict upon which the play begins centers in an attempt to transform the old religious order into a new secular, political one. Perhaps it is a sense of this conflict that prompts Brutus's design for the conspirators as "sacrificers, but not butchers," as "purgers, not murderers": he reverses the initial transformation and attempts to make a political act seem religious. The play's opening upon the Lupercal prepares a way for us to see Brutus's coloring of the assassination in ritualistic images as something other than merely naive or irredeemably evil. It is not a design he has simply made up, but rather one which the transitional atmosphere that hangs over Rome invites him to construct as credible. I shall return to these and similar ideas later; for now, a look at the *Romulus* at least raises questions of where Shakespeare quite literally (or literarily) began.

We cannot be as certain that Shakespeare read the *Romulus* as we are that he read the other three *Lives*, since he does not so overtly "borrow" dialogue and events from it as he does from the others. There is at least one incident in the play, however, that appears only in the *Romulus*. Among the "horrid sights seen by the watch" that forewarn of Caesar's death, Calphurnia describes a vision of "clouds / . . . Which drizzled blood upon the Capitol" (2.2.19–21). There is no such image in the *Lives* of Caesar, Antony, or Brutus, but there is one in the *Romulus*. Plutarch reports a retaliatory ambush by Romulus against the army of neighboring Fidena, after which "there rose suche a great plague in Rome, that men died sodainely, and were not sicke: the earth brought forth no fruite: bruite beasts delivered no increase of their kynde: there rayned also droppes of bloude in Rome, as they saye."

A few pages later, Plutarch describes the meteorological events that accompanied the death of Romulus: "sodainely the weather chaunged, and overcast so terribly, as it is not to be tolde nor credited. For first, the sunne was darckned as if it had bene very night: this darcknes was not in a calme or still, but there fell horrible thunders, boysterous windes, and flashing lightnings on every side, which made the people ronne away . . . but the Senatours kept still close together." Perhaps Shakespeare noted the striking similarity between these descriptions and that which ends the *Life of Caesar:*

> Againe, of signes in the element, the great comet which
> seven nightes together was seene very bright after Caesars
> death, the eight night after was never seene more. Also
> the brightnes of the sunne was darckned, the which all that
> yeare through rose very pale, and shined not out, whereby

it gave but small heate: therefore the ayer being very
clowdy and darke, by the weaknes of the heate that could
not come foorth, did cause the earth to bring foorth but
raw and unrype frute, which rotted before it could rype.

These are doomsday images of the horror of sterility that threatens the welfare of any essentially agrarian state. They suggest the
Waste Land against which purgation and fertility rituals such as the
Lupercalia were invented. They suggest too the plague against which
Marullus warned, and the sense of dis-ease evoked by the play not
only through the repetition of strange portents but also through their
human counterparts: Calphurnia's sterility, Brutus's unaccustomed
estrangement ("Vexed I am / Of late with passions of some difference"—1.2.39–40) and his plea of ill health to stave off Portia's
questions, and Caesar's past and present physical infirmities. People
walk the streets at night in this play, instead of sleeping peacefully,
even though, as Cicero advises, "this disturbed sky / Is not to walk
in"(1.3.38–39). Insomnia holds them; the feeling of disease prevails.
Casca plays dumb: he "puts on this tardy form" (1.2.296) to match
the requirements of the time; and the sick Ligarius arrives at Brutus's
house cloaked in his shroud, anxious for Brutus's "piece of work
that will make sick men whole" (2.1.327). After the assassination,
"Men, wives, and children stare, cry out, and run, / As it were
doomsday" (3.1.97–98).

Other points of connection argue for a reading of the *Romulus*
as a fourth source. We might first consider the fact that Plutarch
describes the Lupercal only in the *Lives* of Romulus and Caesar (and
briefly notes it in connection with Caesar in the *Lives* of Antony and
Augustus). It may be that these references to the festival linked the
two *Lives* in Shakespeare's mind as he read through Plutarch, and
that this link in turn prompted the confluence of images from each
in the play. Several instances in particular suggest parallels in imagery, incident, and design. If these connections are not inescapable,
they are nonetheless quite tempting ones in which Caesar is specifically linked with the Lupercal and with Romulus.

In the *Romulus* we find Caesar mentioned by name, in an episode
which resembles the Fisher-king-Holy Grail type of legend surviving
in the Arthurian romances and celebrated in mumming and sword
dance in Shakespeare's day. The passage also suggests a kind of
atmospheric parallel to the political climate of the play. To test his
strength, Romulus threw a spear made from the wood of a "cornell

tree" from the Aventine to the Palatine. The spear entered so deeply into the ground that no man could pull it out. The soil was quite rich, and the shaft took root and grew branches, and became again "a fayre great cornell tree." Succeeding generations enshrined the tree, enclosing it within a wall and worshipping it "as a very holy thing." Whenever it showed signs of drying out, alarm was spread throughout the community "as if it had bene to have quenched a fyre," and all who heard came running with vessels of water. "In the time of Caius Caesar, who caused the stayers about it to be repayred: they saye the labourers raysing the place, and digging about this cornell tree, dyd by negligence hurte the rootes of the same in suche sorte, as afterwardes it dryed up altogether."

Romulus's cornell tree was not the only structure he planted that later "dried up" under Caius Julius Caesar. One of the last acts of Romulus's life was the establishment of the very system Brutus seeks to preserve in Caesar's Rome. When he inherited control of the city of Alba, in order to "winne the favour of the people there," Romulus "turned the Kingdome to a Comon weale, and every yere dyd chuse a new magistrate to minister justice to the Sabynes. This president taught the noble men of Rome to seeke and desire to have a free estate, where no subject should be at the commaundement of a king alone, and where every man should commaund and obey as should be his course." Under this system, the patricians had no real power, just honorific titles, and were called upon only pro forma in governmental matters. Herein apparently Romulus offended the Senators by acting without their consultation, and now Plutarch's narrative really begins to sound familiar:

> Whereupon the Senatours were suspected afterwards that they killed him, when with in fewe dayes after it was sayed, he vanished away so straungely, that no man ever knewe what became of him. . . . Howbeit, Romulus vanished away sodainely, there was neither seene pece of his garments, nor yet was there found any parte of his body. Therefore some have thought that the whole Senatours fell upon him together in the temple of Vulcan, and how after they had cut him in peces, every one carried away a pece of him, folded close in the skyrte of his robe.

In the end, Romulus's death is accompanied by the same sort of meteorological disturbance that we read of at the end of the *Life of*

Caesar, but further embellished with much frenzied running about and blind credulity on the part of the plebeians, a controlled if somewhat conspiratorial leadership on the part of the Senators, and their elevation of Romulus, to appease the plebs, to the status of a god. And this is where, with Shakespeare's play, we came in.

The cataclysm with which the *Romulus* ends is a prototype of the one that threatens to erupt throughout the first two acts of *Julius Caesar*, does so in the third, and washes over and down through the "domestic fury and fierce civil strife" that Antony promises the "bleeding piece of earth," Caesar's corpse, until the play's end. The "division 'tween our souls" that nearly destroys the friendship of Cassius and Brutus, the disjunction of remorse from power that Brutus fears in Caesar, the insurrection in the state of man that Brutus finds in himself—the play abounds in images of fission within and between individuals as well as in the polis. But the "ambivalent," "ambiguous," and "divided" readings critics find in this "problem play" inhere not only in the behavior of characters or in our responses to them. Ambiguity was in fact a characteristic of Rome under Caesar; the play reflects a fairly accurate sense of the conditions represented in Plutarch's narratives.

The Lupercalian allusions and the various reactions to them in the play illustrate the pervasive and deadly confusion that troubled Rome at this time, a confusion which enabled powerful men like Caesar and Antony to alter the very nature of the state—from republic to empire—and redirect the course of its history. Against that motion, Brutus's effort stands as an impossibly idealistic conservatism, an attempt to hold fast to a Rome that, even as the play begins, is already evaporating. His design for the assassination—that it look like a religious sacrifice—must be seen in the context of the play's Lupercalian opening, for that opening shows how far gone and past recovery the old Rome is.

In 44 B.C., there was a built-in ambivalence in the popular Roman mind about the real meaning and significance of its rituals and traditions. The old Roman sense of time-honored tradition was already lost, perverted to human rather than divine homage. It was at that year's Lupercal that Caesar changed the nature of the festival's observance by adding a new group of priestly celebrants bearing his name (the *Luperci Iulii*) to the traditional two (the *Luperci Fabiani* and *Quintiliani*), and appointed Antony as its leader. This act in turn created the occasion for Antony to offer him the laurel crown "on the Lupercal" (3.2.95), thereby making the holiday a political one in Caesar's honor. As the Lupercal had once been Romulus's festival, so now it became Caesar's. The change in effect elevated Caesar to an equivalence with Romulus, who was deified posthumously. Thus Caesar pretended to both a contraventional Roman "monarchy" and an equally contraventional *living* human "divinity"; Cassius's complaint that "this man / Is now become a god" (1.2.115–16) was entirely justified.

The ambivalence that clouds and subverts the ritual practices of this Rome-in-transition is at the core of several of the play's "ambiguities." Cicero's apothegm that "men may construe things after their fashion, / Clean from the purpose of the things themselves" (1.3.34–35), may indeed be emblematic for the play. It seems that these misconstructions spring from the *particular* misconstruction of ritual and tradition with which the play opens. Misconstruction and misreading are inevitable when the ceremonies that hold a society together and insure its future are suddenly changed or erased. Marullus's altercation with the laborers at the start of the play is only the first instance of this pervasive ambivalence. He represents a remnant of the Old Roman conservatism, and his argument with the workers is his effort to remind them of traditional ritual observance. In this he prefigures Brutus, and like Brutus he fails because the Roman populace has lost touch with the real sacramental import of the ritual. He does not recognize the holiday's transformation from religious to secular and therefore "misconstrues" it. The same conditions allow for the contradictory interpretations of Calphurnia's dream and for the mob's shifting approval first of Brutus's, then of Antony's presentations of the murder. Portia fatally misreads reports of the battle, and Cassius mistakes shouts of victory from Brutus's camp for those of Antony's, leaving Titinius to mourn helplessly: "Alas, thou has misconstrued everything!" (5.3.84). From Cicero's warning to Titinius's cry, the play works out in a circle of misreadings. In this sense too, Brutus "only in a general honest thought / And common good to all made one" of those misconstructions (5.5.71–72).

Such confusions signal the split world of Rome, where the month between the Feast of the Lupercal and the Ides of March comprises the last days and nights of the Republic. The accustomed ground of social, political, and religious practice is cracking open, or so the omens indicate: Casca asks, "Who ever knew the heavens menace so?" and Cassius answers, "Those that have known the earth so full of faults" (1.3.44–45). Within the fissure can be seen the structure of the civilization that underlies the imminently toppling order. It is not only Caesar's death that the play encompasses, or the deaths of the principal conspirators, or that of the poor poet who had the wrong name, or even those of the hundreds of nameless Romans who burned with the city. Besides all these, we witness the end of a political (as well as a religious) order: Caesar's coronation would have signified the end of the Republic, and even his death could not preserve the old order. It is important to remember that all of the prodigies and portents, all of the insomnia, estrangement, and confusion, all the signs of disease are felt and stated *before* Caesar is killed, even before the full conspiracy is mounted. They are not responses to Caesar's death but rather to conditions set in the last months of his life. The disturbance that we mark in the opening scenes of the play is the gathering movement of catastrophe, of the "plague" Marullus warned of, that grows from the events of these last months. The prayer to "intermit the plague" to which Marullus exhorts the carpenter and cobbler should be a prayer for cleansing and purification. The need would have been met by traditional observance of the Lupercalia, but in 44 B.C. such traditions were vitiated and little respected beyond their empty ceremonial forms.

Without proper observance of the appropriate purgative ritual, some other ceremony, or the semblance of one, appears in its place. The imagery of blood sacrifice, so abundant in this play, is more evidence of the perversion of traditional rites. Virtually all of this is Shakespeare's invention: Although Plutarch describes Caesar's assassination vividly, his image is "as a wilde beaste taken of hunters," which of course gives Antony *his* image of Caesar as "a deer, stroken by many princes" (3.1.209). In fact, none of the images in the play that suggest blood sacrifice or ritual of any kind (aside from the references to the Lupercal race) derives from any of the three main *Lives*. Calphurnia's dream of Caesar's statue, "Which, like a fountain with an hundred spouts, / Did run pure blood; and many lusty Romans / Came smiling and did bathe their hands in it" (2.2.77–79), and Decius's flattering interpretation that it "Signifies that from you great Rome shall suck / Reviving blood, and that great men shall press / For tinctures, stains, relics, and cognizance" (2.2.87–89) are both Shakespeare's ideas; Plutarch simply reports the dream as an image of Caesar slain and the statue toppled. Brutus's intention to "carve" Caesar as "a dish fit for the gods," to be "call'd purgers, not murderers" (2.1.174–80), his design to "be sacrificers, but not butchers" (2.1.166), and again his exhortation proving the dream's prophecy: "Stoop, Romans, stoop, / And let us bathe our hands in Caesar's blood / Up to the elbows" (3.1.105–7)—all of these rhetorical images are Shakespeare's embroidery over the plain presentation in Plutarch.

Without any recognizable direct warrant from the three *Lives* for these gory images, critics have tended to assign to them Shakespeare's intention to shock us and to present "the noble Brutus suddenly turned into a savage." It would appear that Shakespeare did invent the bloody hand-washing as part of the process of Caesar's murder, as he seems to have invented the expanded imagery of Calphurnia's dream. But the cutting up of the sacrificial *pharmakos*, whose blood is then smeared upon the flesh of the priestly celebrants, is one of the central events in the rites of the Lupercalia. This is described at length in the *Romulus*:

> Howbeit many things are done, whereof the originall cause were hard now to be conjectured. For goates . . . are killed, then they bring two young boyes, noble mens sonnes, whose foreheads they touch with the knife bebloudied with the bloude of the goates that are sacrificed. By and by they drye their forheads with wolle dipped in milke. Then the yong boyes must laugh immediately after they have dried their forheads. That done they cut the goates skinnes, and make thongs of them, which they take in their hands, and ronne with them all about the cittie.

This passage not only provides a source (or at least an inspiration) for those otherwise inexplicable bloody images—now seen as consistent with and traditional to the fertility aspect of the Lupercalia— but also a context within the play for Brutus's insistence on the semblance of a ritual as the pattern for Caesar's assassination.

It is most interesting in this regard to remember that it is Antony, not Brutus, who is the official Lupercus, and somewhat surprising to realize that, while he opposes Brutus both subtly and actively until the end of the play, he actually seems to endorse the idea that Caesar's death is a sacrifice. It is Antony, not Brutus, who privately addresses Caesar's body as "thou bleeding piece of earth" (3.1.254), and publicly perverts the idea of sacrament for the Romans by making Caesar's body a sacred object:

> Let but the commons hear this testament,
> Which (pardon me) I do not mean to read,
> And they would go and kiss dead Caesar's wounds
> And dip their napkins in his sacred blood;
> Yea, beg a hair of him for memory,
> And dying, mention it within their wills,
> Bequeathing it as a rich legacy
> Unto their issue.
>
> (3.2.130–37)

This new sacramental object will be established by rather question-able means: if the commoners knew (as Antony will soon see to it they shall know) how much money and land Caesar left them, *then* they would sanctify his body. Its "sanctity" is to be bought by giving "To every several man, seventy-five drachmas" (l. 241), and the body itself becomes a property to be passed on "as a rich legacy." The new order, whose shrine is Caesar's corpse, is a duplicitous, mercenary, opportunistic, Machiavellian one. As leader of the Julian Luperci, Antony represents the sacramental system invented by Cae-sar, and he is a far more potent priest than Brutus is. Moreover, he is quite willing to see Rome burn to satisfy his urge to vengeance: "Now let it work. Mischief, thou art afoot, / Take thou what course thou wilt" (3.2.259–60), and content to trade the lives of relatives and friends with the other Triumvirs in the postcataclysmic calm of act 4.

Thus the question that troubles our reading of this play is not whether one can make a murder appear to be a ritual sacrifice. Clearly both pro- and anti-Caesar factions see the popular possibilities in such imagery. The question is rather to what power the "sacrifice" will be made, and in whose interests. Secular politics supplants the old religion, and just as Caesar's blood was offered in libation upon the old altar, so that of the Republic, its people and its ceremonies, will be poured upon the new one. In Antony's curse "upon the limbs of men,"

> Blood and destruction shall be so in use
> And dreadful objects so familiar
> That mothers shall but smile when they behold
> Their infants quartered with the hands of war,
> All pity chok'd with custom of fell deeds.
>
> (3.1.265–69)

The ceremony of purgation and fertility is replaced by one of holocaust, which is no ceremony at all—for ceremonies are by definition orderly and constructively designed toward some idea of fruition. This image is the inverse of ceremony: bloody and destructive.

From its first reference to the variously understood holiday to the last lines of the play, *Julius Caesar* is grounded in this context of ceremonies and rituals: some observed, some ignored, and some twisted to suit particular "celebrants." Such ceremonies are the hallmarks by which we know the values and progresses of whatever civilization we study, and whatever else this play may appear to signify, at its most literal it is the story of "what Shakespeare and his audience regarded as one of the great dramatic events in the history of the world"; the play "alludes to many formal ceremonies, ranging from the 'order of the course' and the ceremonies of the Lupercal . . . to the 'respect and rites of burial' which are due Brutus at the end of the play. . . . But ceremony pervades the world of the play; if Brutus is a ritualist he is in harmony with his culture."

The social rituals traced within the play occur within the larger context of the Lupercalia as a perennially observed religious ritual. And it is within this larger context that the conservative Brutus operates. His desire to make Caesar's murder seem ritualistic is not the same thing as an attempt to make it an *actual* ritual, nor does he say anywhere outside the confidential circle of conspirators that it is one. His orations to the people (3.2.12–46) contain no references to ritual—although, as we have seen, Antony's do—but only political justifications to the commons' sense of republicanism. The image that Brutus seeks to create is not, therefore, impossible; it is not even unlikely. It is entirely consistent with what he believes (and Antony proves) to be an acceptable avenue to public approbation. What, then, went wrong?

Brutus's errors, including his reluctance to kill Antony and his permission for Antony to speak (and speak last) at Caesar's funeral, have been noted by nearly every critic since Plutarch himself pointed them out. As I have already suggested, several of the play's characters understand the world imperfectly. Brutus does not err, however, in seeing Caesar's arrogance as a threat to the Republic; Caesar's language and actions in the play just before the assassination show that Brutus's fears are well founded, and even Plutarch asserts, in the *Life of Caesar*, that "the chiefest cause that made him mortally hated, was the covetous desire he had to be called king: which first gave the people just cause, and next his secret enemies, honest colour to beare him ill will." Nor is Brutus wrong in trying to use a familiar ritualistic paradigm to encourage his friends in their sense of the justice of their conspiracy. Brutus's central error, the "efficient cause" in his failure to preserve the Republic, consists mainly in his simply human inability to predict the consequences of the very history of which he is himself an agent.

"History" is, of course, rarely clear to those for whom it is still the present; perhaps only soothsayers and manipulators like Antony have the skill to foresee the future. Brutus does understand the history of the age preceding his own. Cassius reminds him of the Rome that was:

> When could they say (till now) that talk'd of Rome
> That her wide walks encompass'd but one man?
> Now is it Rome indeed, and room enough,
> When there is in it but one only man!
> O, you and I have heard our fathers say
> There was a Brutus once that would have brook'd
> Th'eternal devil to keep his state in Rome
> As easily as a king.
>
> (1.2.154–61)

And Brutus later reminds himself: "My ancestors did from the streets of Rome / The Tarquin drive when he was call'd a king" (2.1.53–54). He is persuaded best by arguments that refer to the past, to tradition, and especially to family traditions, as in the lines above and again in Portia's appeal to him to share his troubles with her: she is "stronger than [her] sex" (2.1.295–97) because she is Cato's daughter. It is Brutus's sense of history that enables him to identify the "tide in the affairs of men" that governs their successes in the world. The problem is that, as he continues,

> On such a full sea are we now afloat,
> And we must take the current when it serves
> Or lose our ventures.
>
> (4.3.222–24)

Unfortunately Brutus misses *his* current (meaning both the watery force and the sense of the immediate present that the word simultaneously connotes): his hamartia is, quite literally, a "missing of the mark."

As Norman Rabkin [in *Shakespeare and the Common Understanding*] and others have noted, the "tide in the affairs of men" that this play describes is specifically one of human political history. That tide is inevitably repetitive, if not altogether cyclical, as is suggested at several points in the play. Caesar triumphed over Pompey and died under his image, at the foot of Pompey's statue; Brutus in turn dies with the image of Caesar in his mind's eye: "Caesar, now be still" (5.5.50). Antony's eulogy over Caesar as the "noblest man / That ever lived in the tide of times" (3.1.256–57) echoes in his final praise of Brutus as "the noblest Roman of them all" (5.5.68). When Cassius reminds Brutus that "there was a Brutus once," the present Brutus remembers that he too has a cycle to repeat. The movement, or the moving, of history is the process in evidence in *Julius Caesar*, and Cassius's cryptic prophecy that in "many ages hence / Shall this our lofty scene be acted over" (3.1.111–12) merely lends a particularly theatrical self-consciousness to what is otherwise a neat acknowledgment of the recurrent politics of human history.

Ultimately the tide in the affairs of men has its own impetus, often stronger than and indifferent to individual human will. Once initiated, events are answered with consequent events. "The evil that men do lives after them" not only in Antony's sense of reputation but also in the historical sense of repercussion: an act of tyranny calls for one of liberation; assassination in turn is answered by revenge, and so on. The tide whose current Brutus misses becomes a flood of anarchy, of the "mutiny" Antony calls into being (3.2.209). The play offers other metaphors for this action: the "dogs of war" will be unleashed (3.1.273), and mischief, once afoot, will indeed take its own course (3.2.259–60). Antony understands this perfectly; Brutus never tells us whether he does.

Brutus is not so much naive as he is old-fashioned, out of time as it progresses over and around him. He does not seem to realize that he cannot stop the flow of events. His action is as heroic as it is futile. In the play's final analysis, he is "the noblest Roman of them all"; more specifically, he is the noblest Roman of the Rome that was. The Empire that succeeded it was never to touch its glory. The picture Shakespeare gives us of the Triumvirate is a sickening image: Octavius, Antony, and Lepidus coldly trading names and lives of relatives and friends marked for annihilation. And whereas Brutus's committee of conspirators, in the parallel scene in 2.1., honestly and honorably excludes men like Cicero who cannot be counted on to support their united effort, the Triumvirate itself is a sham perpetrated by Antony and followed by Octavius. They will use Lepidus to "ease ourselves of divers sland'rous loads" and then "turn him off / (Like to the empty ass) to shake his ears / And graze in commons" (4.1.20–27). These three are the leaders of the Rome that is left smoldering after the commons, themselves ignited by Antony's careful rhetoric, fire the city and slaughter the unfortunate poet with the wrong name. The Rome that Brutus hopes for is perverted into a self-devouring creature (anticipating perhaps Albany's prediction in *King Lear* that "humanity must perforce prey on itself, / Like monsters of the deep"—4.2.49–50), and the intended purgative and regenerative ritual becomes the mere anarchy of bacchanalian frenzy. Ironically for Brutus, Caesar's blood could never have nourished a land far too desiccated by opportunistic corruption to profit by such remedy; it is simply absorbed into the earth.

We have access to past civilizations and cultures primarily through two kinds of records: those of historical or singular events and those of traditional or repeated ones, such as rituals. In reading Plutarch, Shakespeare certainly found both kinds of records. But Shakespeare's interest was surely not that of the historian, folklorist, or any other kind of scholar. Whatever prompted him to incorporate and apply those images and occasions he recalled from the *Romulus*, it had to have been for the sake of theatrical texture, not scholarship. He had to know that the patterns and concerns of his play matched those of his audience, who undoubtedly did not share our modern delight in footnotes and esoterica. Thanks to a number of recent critical studies, not to mention the evidence of the plays themselves, it is hardly necessary to restate the obvious fact that Shakespeare's audience was generally interested in Roman history and its major figures. In all of his Roman plays, Shakespeare was [as T. J. B. Spencer pointed out] "producing a mimesis of the veritable history of the most important people (humanly speaking) who ever lived, the concern of every educated man in Europe and not merely something of local, national, patriotic interest."

A very strong concern for historical verisimilitude might urge a playwright toward so complete a mimesis that he includes in his play even ritual practices already dying out in the culture his play presents. But neither *Julius Caesar* nor any other work of his suggests that Shakespeare had any such compulsion to observe minutiae of that sort, nor, we may suppose, did the bulk of his audience. Yet these elements are consciously and effectively woven into this play, and clearly with an artist's skill for representation rather than a schoolmaster's penchant for didacticism. On what grounds may we suggest that Shakespeare would have been interested in the rituals of a decaying Roman religion, and further, how could he have counted on his audience's reception and comprehension of the issues they express?

However sophisticated and secular it may have been, the life of a Londoner in Shakespeare's time was in many respects ordered by rituals both civic and ecclesiastic. His plays frequently reflect the importance of that combined ordering as law and religion, the two faces of human governance. For example, in *The Merchant of Venice* (quite distant from *Julius Caesar* in genre and style, but only about three years earlier in composition), the two strains intersect at several points, and most strikingly in a perverse image at the moment of Bassanio's casket-choosing:

> In law, what plea so tainted and corrupt
> But being season'd with a gracious voice,
> Obscures the show of evil? In religion,
> What damned error but some sober brow
> Will bless it and approve it with a text
> Hiding the grossness with fair ornament?
> (3.2.75–80)

These lines concentrate for us the full context in which the play's action occurs, the major bonds by which society regulates itself in an ordered and self-perpetuating system. The interrelation of these bonds is in a sense the nexus of Shakespeare's world, powerfully evident in the civic and ecclesiastic festivals of London as well as in the much older and lasting seasonal celebrations of his native Warwickshire. Such concerns were part of every Elizabethan's life: they were not only historically but perennially significant.

Certain features of the festivals celebrated by both urban and rural Elizabethans offer tantalizing prospects for any of the following suppositions: that *Julius Caesar*'s incorporation of Lupercalian elements would have struck familiar chords for its audience; that the play's concerns with right rule and order, and their passage, are essentially the same as those of many folk and civic festivals generally; that Shakespeare's familiarity with the rural practices of various festivals in Warwickshire sensitized him to the analogous rites he read about in Plutarch. In the terms of the "network of analogies and parallels" that Maurice Charney suggests, these English rites pretty well ensured his audience's comprehension of those elements in the play in more or less precisely the same context: as necessary guarantors, whether pagan or Christian, ecclesiastic or secular, rural or civic, of order, succession, and fruition in the realm.

In Warwickshire particularly, Lupercalia-like rites were followed. The most remarkably similar custom—"Beating the Bounds"—was practiced throughout England. For Warwickshire, it has been described in this way [by Margaret Baker]:

> Walking the parish boundaries . . . was an essential part of parish administration before maps and literacy were commonplace. . . . At the boundary marks (a tree, a stone, a pond) the parson paused to give thanks for the fruits of the earth and to read the gospel. . . . The company, carrying peeled willow wands, then turned to the boys and, more or less severely according to the period, beat and bumped them or pushed them in a nearby stream, all excellent reminders of boundaries.

Whatever their didactic value, the resemblance of these practices to the Lupercalian race around the city of Rome and the thong-lashing is worth noting. The timing of these customs in England seems to vary by village: at Stratford, for instance, they occurred in the spring, but elsewhere in Warwickshire, at Warwick, Ilmington, and Birmingham, the custom was specifically a Michaelmas tradition. And although Stratford did not "beat the bounds" at Michaelmas, the town was otherwise engaged in what is called the "most famous" of its Michaelmas traditions, the Stratford Hiring or "Mop" Fair, which served as a marketplace or labor-exchange for hiring farmhands and housemaids (hence, the "mop" or sign of the profession). The Stratford Mop was almost always accompanied by Morris dancing and a variation on the Hobbyhorse dance called "Grinning"—a contest in which the "frightfullest grinner [through a horse collar was] to be winner."

The forms and functions of Morris, sword, and Hobbyhorse dances, and their appearances and semblances in his work, are happily familiar to most students of Shakespeare, and need not be recounted here. And although significant attention has been given to the Roman Saturnalia as analogous to these seasonal folk practices in England, the equally close relation of the Lupercalia has not been recognized. Indeed, some elements of these festivals may be better understood by reference to the Lupercalia than to the Saturnalia. Besides the mildly violent boundary-running, there is for instance the whipping of the spectators by the Fool during the Morris, which is in effect the inverse of the Saturnalian scapegoat sacrifice and more closely resembles the flagellation of the Lupercal-race. The Hobbyhorse too is related to the fertility aspects of the Lupercalia, whenever, as in Cornwall, it chases and traps the village girls under its hood. To be so caught was considered a sign of luck, and especially of fecundity. On occasion, the "Horse" would "smear its captives' faces with tar or soot as part of the initiation process." This last act recalls the equally unexplained blood-smearing initiation of the Lupercalia, which may in turn have been reflected in the grotesque bloodbath scenes, including Antony's handshake, in *Julius Caesar*.

Although they might seem both dramatically and historically distancing, set off in a world more than one and a half millennia away, the rites and signs of the Lupercal would almost certainly have seemed culturally familiar to Shakespeare's audience. They need not have known that these were specifically *Roman* rites; they need only have understood what the rites symbolized in their own terms, what urges, necessities, fears, or assurances they stood for. Such recognition is by no means the exclusive business of the educated classes; echoes of domestic practices may prompt constructive associations in the mind of any viewer. And while I would not in this case argue for the same intensity of correlation which R. Chris Hassel, Jr., urges for the courtly audience's recognition of English liturgical elements in other plays, his conjecture that they "would probably . . . have noticed and enjoyed parallels that we have missed completely" is one I think we can reasonably apply to the ritualistic elements in *Julius Caesar*. We cannot know whether Shakespeare worked the Lupercalian elements into his play to create an accurate representation of historical and political Rome, a resonant semblance of native English rites to assist the audience's identification, or yet another thematic thread to bind the play's complexity. But his use of them in this play is, as I have tried to show, definite and deliberate, and should be considered whenever we return—as the critical disagreements promise we shall do—to wonder what he really had in mind.

Rhetoric in Ancient Rome

Anne Barton

On the eve of Caesar's assassination, when the heavens rain down fire and Rome is filled with prodigies and portents, Casca encounters Cicero in the streets. Breathless and dismayed, Casca pours out a tale of marvels, abnormalities which, he believes, must prefigure some calamity to the state. Cicero, who remains icily calm, admits that

> Indeed, it is a strange-disposed time;
> But men may construe things after their fashion,
> Clean from the purpose of the things themselves.
>
> (1.3.33–35)

For Elizabethans, this warning of how language may misrepresent fact, how words—whether involuntarily or on purpose—can falsify phenomenal experience, must have seemed especially striking on the lips of Cicero: acknowledged grand master of the art of persuasion, the greatest orator and rhetorician of the ancient world. Shakespeare's Cicero makes no attempt himself to interpret the terrors of the night. He rests content with the neutral observation that disturbed skies such as these are not to walk in, then leaves the stage. In the very next moment, Cassius enters and Casca finds himself confronting a man who proceeds at once to construe things "clean from the purpose of the things themselves" and, what is more, makes Casca believe

---

From *Shakespeare's Craft: Eight Lectures*, edited by Philip H. Highfill, Jr. © 1982 by The George Washington University. Southern Illinois University Press, 1982.

him. By the end of the scene, Casca has not only accepted Cassius's very different view of the tempest as a reflection of the diseased and monstrous condition of Rome under Caesar's rule, he has agreed as a result to join the conspirators and end that rule through an act of violence. In doing so, he helps to bring about precisely that cataclysm, that condition of anarchy and upheaval that, initially, he feared.

Although Cicero has no part in the action of *Julius Caesar*, it seems to have been important to Shakespeare that the audience should, from time to time, be reminded of his presence and of the controversy associated with his name. In the second scene of act 1, Cicero passes across the stage twice as a member of Caesar's entourage. Brutus as bystander remarks on the discontent in his eyes. Casca says that after Antony's abortive effort to crown Caesar, Cicero spoke in Greek and that those who understood him smiled and shook their heads. In act 2, after the scene with Casca, Cicero's name is introduced again when Brutus insists upon overruling his confederates and excluding him from the conspiracy on the highly suspect grounds that "he will never follow anything / That other men begin." At Sardis, in act 4, Cassius is shocked to learn that Cicero was one of the senators proscribed by the triumvirs and that he is dead. It is a scattered collection of references but, I believe, purposeful. By keeping the enormous memory of Cicero alive in his tragedy, Shakespeare constantly directs his audience's attention towards Rome as the city of orators and rhetoricians: a place where the art of persuasion was cultivated, for better or for worse, to an extent unparalleled in any other society.

The argument over the ethical status of oratory begins long before the time of Cicero. In the *Gorgias*, Plato allowed Socrates to tear the rhetoricians to shreds, on the grounds that their art creates spurious belief without instructing either the listeners or the practitioner in the nature of the Good. It is really a way of managing ignorant mankind through flattery and so not an art at all, properly considered, but an equivocal skill existing in the same relationship to the soul that elaborate cookery does to the body: the rhetorician makes things taste so nice that we swallow them whole, without inquiring into the true nature of the ingredients. Aristotle tried to rescue rhetoric from Plato's scorn. He made his own verdict that it was a genuine art quite plain by writing a treatise on the subject himself and by insisting upon its close relationship with the truth-finding science of Logic. Aristotle's *Rhetoric*, although it was to exert a powerful influence on Renaissance theories of style, nonetheless managed to provide the enemy with valuable ammunition by admitting that the justification of the orator's art lies in the fact that an ignorant and uneducated public is incapable of distinguishing truth from falsehood through the exercise of reason and therefore needs to be persuaded through an appeal to faculties other than the rational. This, of course, is all very well provided that the orator himself can tell good from evil, *and* happens to be an honest man. But what if he is not? Montaigne, whose contempt for the arts of persuasion was positively withering, made use of Aristotle in his own assault upon the rhetoricians. Oratory, he asserted, in his essay "On the Vanitie of Words," is a cozening and deceitful art devised "to busie, to manage, and to agitate a vulgar and disordered multitude." In states where

> the vulgar, the ignorant, or the generalities have had all the power, as that of Rhodes, those of Athens and that of Rome, and where things have ever beene in continuall disturbance and uproare, thither have Orators and professors of that Art flocked.

The crucial position of Cicero in this venerable argument is the result not only of his colossal reputation as the great orator/statesman of antiquity and the creator of a model prose style: it derives from his attempt to demonstrate, both in his writing and in his own political career, that Plato's gulf between rhetoric and philosophy could be closed—that the great orator must also be a virtuous man and his art dedicated to the service of truth and right action. On the whole, Cicero emerges well from the scrutiny of Plutarch. He seems to have been physically timid; he was childishly vain of his own abilities and achievements and given to the kind of personal sarcasm that makes needless enemies, but his essential probity and his concern for the welfare and continuance of the Roman republic are never in doubt. Yet, even with Cicero, it is clear that precept and practice were not always in accord. Plutarch records that he once turned on a former client with the taunt: "Do you suppose you were acquitted for your own merits, Munatius, and was it not that I so darkened the case, that the court could not see your guilt?" For all his protestations to the contrary, Cicero was not above exercising his eloquence for its own sake, in defense of what he knew to be a bad cause. The anti-

Ciceronian movement of the Renaissance was essentially stylistic in its concerns, but at least some of its adherents (notably Montaigne) reacted against Cicero's ornate prose precisely because those long, periodic sentences, with their hypnotic rhythms and massed, parallel clauses, seemed to them glib and insincere, an elevation of manner over matter in which truth was neglected or submerged.

Shakespeare's friend Ben Jonson was a notable anti-Ciceronian, a man who modeled his own prose on the curt and deliberately inharmonious style of Tacitus and Seneca. Despite this aesthetic predilection, he wrote a tragedy in which Cicero appears not as the background figure that he was in Shakespeare's *Julius Caesar* but as the hero. Jonson's *Catiline* (1611) also examines the Roman world of words, but it conducts this examination in a narrow and specialized way. The real gloss on *Catiline* is provided by Francis Bacon's little book, *Of the Colours of Good and Evil* (1597), a treatise designed to instruct readers in the difference between honest and dishonest rhetorical argument. Bacon, himself (of course) a distinguished orator, believed as strongly as Cicero that rhetoric, the science of moving the will, ought to be tied to the service of truth. As a political realist he was aware, however, that all too often it was not. Hence his desire to expose the tricks of the trade, to demonstrate how things in themselves good or evil may be colored by the skillful orator until they look like their opposites.

Jonson's *Catiline* is a kind of dramatic version of Bacon's *Colours of Good and Evil*. The action of the play, if you can call it that, consists almost entirely of a comparison of Cicero's style of persuasion with that of the villainous Catiline. Jonson's Cicero is no angel. He makes use of informers, administers bribes, doesn't always tell the truth, and occasionally acts outside the law. The political game in Rome enforces compromise of this kind. He is able, nonetheless, to save the republic: not only because he is intelligent, dedicated, and essentially honest, but because he can give these particular personal qualities a persuasive, linguistic shape. Although Cicero is what his enemies like to call an upstart consul, a new man not of senatorial rank, he makes words take the place of wealth, family, and influential connections. Catiline, superficially, is an effective speaker too. But Jonson is determined to show that for the intelligent auditor, the listener who also thinks, all of Catiline's arguments simply give him away for the man he is: false, violent, greedy, hysterical, and entirely destructive. To move from Catiline's speeches to those of Cicero is to exchange false rhetoric for true in a sense that Bacon and (for that matter) the historical Cicero would have understood.

The Elizabethans did not applaud Jonson's *Catiline*. Like its predecessor *Sejanus* (1603), Jonson's second Roman tragedy failed on the stage. It is difficult, for all the wit and intelligence of the play, not to sympathize with this original verdict. *Catiline* explores an issue as important in modern as in ancient political life, but it is curiously academic and circumscribed. Encumbered by Jonson's learning, and by a certain inflexibility and didacticism in its handling of the past, it is so much drama à *thèse* that it almost ceases to be drama at all. Jonson's original audience apparently liked the first two acts, tolerated the third, and broke into open revolt when asked to attend to Cicero's culminating oration—all three-hundred-odd lines of it—in act 4. It is tempting to believe that Shakespeare was at least partly to blame. After all, by 1611 London audiences had already seen *Julius Caesar* and *Coriolanus:* two tragedies which also focus on persuasion, on the pleasures and perils of rhetoric in ancient Rome, but which do so in a fashion not only far more dramatic than Jonson's but more wide-ranging, provocative and profound.

In the Rome of *Coriolanus*, rhetoric is often a highly dubious commodity. Menenius, Volumnia, the tribunes, and the Volscian Aufidius all use it upon occasion to falsify fact. Nevertheless, tricky and dangerous though they are, words are still the necessary tools with which a society is built and maintained. To reject the arts of persuasion out of hand, to minimize language, is to become either as passive and limited in one's activities as Virgilia or else a lonely dragon like Coriolanus himself. This is especially true in a society like the one presented in this play: a Rome which is in the process of developing new and more sophisticated values and political forms. These new ideas and structures are, to a large extent, the creation of language: the product of argument and discussion among human beings. Rhetoric, in this process, has an honest as well as a suspect part to play. It was only when he wrote about the later republic, about a city become stagnant, its democratic institutions corrupt and decayed, that Shakespeare treated Roman oratory as something unequivocally poisonous: the ruin both of individuals and of the state.

Although *Julius Caesar* was written eight or nine years before *Coriolanus*, the Rome it depicts is historically much later: a dying republic that has outlived its earlier vitality and is about to collapse into some kind of dictatorship, whether that of Caesar or Octavius. It is a city of professional persuaders. Brutus and Cassius are even unable to have a private quarrel without a lunatic poet, that neither of them has ever seen before, bursting into the tent unannounced to urge, grandiloquently, that they "Love and be friends, as two such men should be." This, in effect, is the kind of democracy about which Montaigne was so scathing, where things are in "continuall disturbance and uproare," and orators and teachers of that art take advantage of the power they have over a fickle and disordered multitude. Montaigne regarded this syndrome as a powerful argument in favor of monarchy.

> For, that foolishnesse and facilitie, which is found in the common multitude, and which doth subject the same, to be managed, perswaded, and led by the eares, by the sweet alluring and sense-entrancing sound of this harmonie, without duly weighing, knowing, or considering the trueth of things by the force of reason: This facultie and easie yeelding, I say, is not so easily found in one only ruler, and it is more easie to warrant him from the impression of this poyson, by good institution and sound counsell.

It is interesting to note, in the light of Montaigne's belief, that Shakespeare's Caesar sees his own greatness partly in terms of his unpersuadability. Constant as the northern star, "that unassailable holds on his rank, / Unshak'd of motion," his blood—or so he claims—cannot "be thaw'd from the true quality / With that which melteth fools—I mean sweet words." In point of fact, Caesar has not escaped the general malaise of his city. He is present, fatally, in the Senate to speak these words only because he has been persuaded by Decius Brutus that, looked at properly, Calphurnia's ominous dream is flattering and propitious. Not until the final section of the tragedy does the genuinely unpersuadable man make his appearance. Shakespeare waited on the whole until *Antony and Cleopatra* to examine the character traits of Octavius, but the outline is already clear in the earlier play.

> ANTONY: Octavius, lead your battle softly on
>   Upon the left hand of the even field.
> OCTAVIUS: Upon the right hand I. Keep thou the left.

ANTONY: Why do you cross me in this exigent?
OCTAVIUS: I do not cross you; but I will do so.

End of argument.

Julius Caesar, like *Coriolanus*, opens with a scene of persuasion. The Roman citizens in this play, however, are entirely passive: mere puppets manipulated by others. They do not engage in debate as their equivalents do in *Coriolanus*, neither among themselves nor with the tribune Flavius. The cobbler, the carpenter, and their associates arrive in holiday attire, intending to shout themselves hoarse at great Caesar's triumph. When Flavius has finished speaking to them, they vanish ("tongue-tied," as he says contemptuously) to their homes, obscurely certain without any reasons having been advanced that Caesar is a bad thing, while Pompey was somehow splendid. They will reverse themselves quite as irrationally in act 2, with far more serious consequences, when Brutus makes the tactical mistake of permitting Mark Antony to speak last—the position which the historical Cicero always advocated—in Caesar's funeral.

Public oratory in *Julius Caesar* is slick and professional as it never is in *Coriolanus*. Flavius, unlike Menenius, has been reading textbooks in the art of rabble-rousing. With its carefully spaced rhetorical questions, deceptive logic, emotive vocabulary, and hypnotic repetitions—"And do you now put on your best attire? / And do you now cull out a holiday? / And do you now strew flowers"—his speech is calculated to drown reason in passion. So, of course, is Antony's even more accomplished appeal to the crowd later on. Nonetheless, although Antony immediately turns the mutiny he has stirred up to his own political advantage—even truncating those legacies to the people of which he had made such capital in describing Caesar's will—he does at least share some of the emotion that he arouses in others on behalf of Caesar dead. "That I did love thee, Caesar, O, 'tis true." Flavius's tears for Pompey, on the other hand, are purely crocodilian. His real reason for tampering with the citizens emerges only after they have slunk guiltily off the stage:

> These growing feathers pluck'd from Caesar's wing
> Will make him fly an ordinary pitch,
> Who else would soar above the view of men
> And keep us all in servile fearfulness.

This is the hidden but real issue, not only of Flavius's speech but of much of the play.

Almost all the talk about democracy, freedom, tyranny, and restraint in *Julius Caesar* is really a camouflage for something else. Shakespeare's Caesar happens to be deaf in one ear, childless, subject to epileptic fits, vain, superstitious, and as likely to drown in a wintry river or succumb to a fever as soon as any other mortal. Despite these obvious shortcomings, he is also a Colossus: a man over life-size who has created and can control an empire. Cassius says angrily that "this man / Is now become a god," but the real difficulty is that he has not. Gods, after all, are exempt from our envy precisely because they belong to a different order of being. Competition is out of the question, and so is the kind of jealousy that springs from a resented inferiority. Caesar's various human failings are really more exacerbating than his genius, because they remind lesser men, running in the same race with the same handicaps, that they have been far outstripped. Cassius articulates this response most fully, but it is one that many other Roman patricians share, not least—as Cassius knows—the noble Brutus.

In *Julius Caesar*, the art of persuasion has come to permeate life so completely that people find themselves using it not only to influence others but to deceive themselves. This is true, above all, of Brutus. Brutus is competent enough as a public orator, although he lacks the fire and subtlety of Mark Antony, but his real verbal ingenuity declares itself only when he is using the techniques of oratory to blind himself and (occasionally) his friends. In the orchard soliloquy of act 2, Brutus extracts purpose and resolve not from the facts of the situation but from a collection of verbal nothings: from words like "may" and "would." There is no tangible basis for Brutus's fears of Caesar. Indeed, as he admits, observation and circumstance suggest the contrary. He is driven, as a result, to do the thing for which he secretly longs—kill Caesar—purely on the basis of a grammatical construction: a verbal emptiness which pretends to have the status of a fact. "Then lest he may, prevent." Antony had said of Caesar earlier in the play that his words were precisely equivalent to deeds: "When Caesar says, 'Do this,' it is performed." Brutus too tries to blur the distinction between speech and action, but the effect he creates is one of self-delusion rather than power.

Shakespeare's Caesar likes to refer to himself in the third person. "Speak, Caesar is turned to hear," he says to the soothsayer in act 1, and in later scenes he resorts to this kind of self-naming almost obsessively. Shakespeare knew, of course, that the historical Caesar had written his commentary on the Gallic Wars in the third person, but there is more behind the mannerism (with Caesar as with General de Gaulle in our own time) than a mere literary practice. Self-naming implies taking oneself very seriously. It is a deliberately grand way of regarding one's own identity, as though that identity were already matter for historians. Antony is never guilty of it in *Julius Caesar*. He delivers all of his great oration in the first person. Brutus, by contrast, not only employs this peculiarly Roman form of the royal "we" in his defense to the citizens, he uses the third person repeatedly in private conversation. "Brutus," he tells Cassius, "had rather be a villager / Than to repute himself a son of Rome / Under these hard conditions." The effect of these persistent presentations of Brutus by Brutus as a somehow externalized object is to suggest that, although this man is in many ways noble, he is also far too aware of the fact. Indeed, it suggests an underlying affinity with Caesar: the man Brutus kills, supposedly, because Caesar was ambitious.

Cassius plays upon this failing. His persuasion is as deadly as it is because it recognizes and takes advantage of a deeply buried jealousy of Caesar, lurking behind all of Brutus's avowed republican principles, a jealousy which happens to be less conscious than his own. He harps upon Brutus as public figure, the cynosure of every eye, whose ancestors drove the kings from Rome: a man whose scope and potentialities for greatness have somehow been cabined, cribb'd, confin'd by the rival presence of Caesar. He makes Brutus feel that he must commit a spectacular public act in order to validate his name. In doing this, Cassius is less than honest. His victim, however, not only plays into his hands but betters his instruction.

In the orchard soliloquy of act 2, Brutus turned the techniques of oratory against his own conscience. He continues to do this throughout the remainder of the play. The man who pretends, in act 4, that he does not know about his wife's death, purely in order to impress Messala with the superhuman fortitude of the hero encountering pain, also tries to delude himself that the conspiracy is a kind of holy league. This is why he refuses to countenance an oath to bind its members. Even worse, he uses language dishonestly (much as Othello does after him) when he tries to persuade the conspirators that Caesar's death will be not a butchery but a religious sacrifice:

> We all stand up against the spirit of Caesar,
> And in the spirit of men there is no blood.
> O, that we then could come by Caesar's spirit,
> And not dismember Caesar.

They must, he claims, be "called purgers, not murderers." The names make all the difference.

In the event, the spirit of Caesar is precisely the thing they do not kill. They merely release it from the shackles of its human form and failings. No longer deaf, arrogant, epileptic, or subject to error, this spirit walks abroad as a thing against which, now, there is no defense. At Philippi, it turns the swords of the conspirators into their own proper entrails. It raises up a successor in the form of Octavius, who will annihilate the republic in Rome. Even before this happens, Brutus's appeal to the transforming power of words has become half desperate. In the spirit of men there is no blood. But blood, in the first scene of act 3, is the element in which the conspirators are drenched. It dyes all of them scarlet, sticks to hands as well as to daggers, disgustingly daubs their faces and their clothes. Not even Brutus can pretend not to notice the sheer physical mess. Characteristically, he tries to spiritualize it, to alter its character by linguistic means:

> Stoop, Romans, stoop,
> And let us bathe our hands in Caesar's blood
> Up to the elbows, and besmear our swords:
> Then walk we forth, even to the market-place,
> And waving our red weapons o'er our heads,
> Let's all cry, "Peace, freedom, and liberty!"

Blood is not blood, he insists, but purely symbolic. It stands for the idea of freedom. The euphemism, and the action with which it is connected, is one of which the second half of the twentieth century has heard all too much.

Like Coriolanus, Brutus ends almost where he began. Rome moves on, and leaves both men behind. The last words of Brutus are not furious, like those of Coriolanus, but they are equally hard to accept. "In all my life," he says proudly, "I found no man but he was true to me." In Shakespeare, although not in Plutarch, Messala has already defected to Caesar, as Strato bitterly points out. Nor will time to come necessarily endorse Brutus's last vision of himself: a vision in which, characteristically, he is still presenting himself in the third person.

> I shall have glory by this losing day
> More than Octavius and Mark Antony
> By this vile conquest shall attain unto.
> So fare you well at once; for Brutus' tongue
> Hath almost ended his life's history.

Dante, after all, placed Brutus beside Judas Iscariot in the seventh circle of Hell.

Antony, as one might expect, is generous. "This was the noblest Roman of them all." He leaves us with the image of a Brutus who was gentle, devoid of envy, and perfectly temperate and well balanced: not at all the Brutus who was vulnerable to the persuasions of Cassius, the rash and intemperate man of the quarrel in act 4, who gave the word too early at Philippi. "In your bad strokes, Brutus, you give good words," Antony had said shrewdly before. He forgets these criticisms now. Funeral orations tend, of course, to be false— whether out of good will and compassion for the dead, or because it seems necessary now to tidy everything up in accordance with the demands of piety and decorum. "Let's make the best of it," one of the Volscian lords urges at the end of *Coriolanus,* after Aufidius and the crowd have with some difficulty been made to stop trampling on the body. Even Aufidius, the man who planned and executed Coriolanus's murder in the coldest of cold blood, announces penitently that his rage is gone, "and I am struck with sorrow." Here, especially, the rhetoric rings false. Antony's encomium on the dead Brutus comes nearer truth, but it is far from satisfactory or complete. The meanings inherent in the stories of Coriolanus and of Brutus cannot be extracted from funeral orations. They require language of another kind: language that is both further from the facts of the situation and, in another sense, closer. Plato did not like the poets any more than he did the actors and rhetoricians. Nevertheless, it is in Shakespeare's two Roman plays that the truth about Brutus and Coriolanus now seems to live.

The Roman Actor: *Julius Caesar*

Jonathan Goldberg

> *Some Parallel'd him to* Tiberius *for Dissimulation, yet Peace was*
> *maintained by him as in the Time of* Augustus: *And Peace begot Plenty,*
> *and Plenty begot Ease and Wantonness, and Ease and Wantonness begot*
> *Poetry, and Poetry swelled to that Bulk in his time, that it begot strange*
> *Monstrous Satyrs against the King's own Person.*
> ARTHUR WILSON, Life and Reign of James I

Dismissing the conspirators, Brutus gives them this final piece of
advice:

> Good gentlemen, look fresh and merrily.
> Let not our looks put on our purposes,
> But bear it as our Roman actors do,
> With untired spirits and formal constancy.
>
> (2.1.224–27)

Brutus is instructing the conspirators in the acts of duplicity, yet
there is a contradiction in the lines that surpasses those that we may
suppose Brutus intends. Inviting the conspirators to disguise purposes in pleasant looks, Brutus calls for them to put on a "look"
even as he asks them not to have their "looks put on our purposes."
This contradiction is sustained in the attitude toward acting that
underlies the passage. Assuming the "untired spirits and formal constancy" of Roman actors, the duplicity of the conspirators is invested

---

From *James I and the Politics of Literature: Jonson, Shakespeare, Donne, and Their*
Contemporaries. © 1983 by The Johns Hopkins University Press, Baltimore/London.

in an imagined form of resplendent transcendence. The Roman actor, untired, formal, constant, has all the permanence of Roman representation, lively statues. The duplicitous form of the actor, masking purposes in a look that is not seen, a look that is not "looks," achieves the permanent form of a spirit. This is not only the form of an actor, it is also, quite simply, the form of power in the play. It is how Caesar sees himself:

> I could be well moved, if I were as you;
> If I could pray to move, prayers would move me:
> But I am constant as the Northern Star,
> Of whose true-fixed and resting quality
> There is no fellow in the firmament.
>
> (3.1.58–62)

This is what Caesar would be. A moment later hands speak, and the drama in Pompey's Theater issues in the savage spectacle of Caesar, bleeding beneath Pompey's statue.

We need to pause over that moment in a theater, and over Brutus's injunction to his fellow actors, for ideas fundamental to action on the stage of history (as fundamental as that metaphor) seem at issue. Why does Brutus conceive of the action of the conspiracy as a theatrical event? Why does it occur in Pompey's Theater? To answer fully those questions, we will need to look beyond *Julius Caesar* . . . [at] a number of Roman plays of the Jacobean period. It is no accident that we can look there for representations that bear on the nature of history and the understanding of power in this time. James had placed a Roman stamp on his reign; that was the "style of gods" he claimed with imperial precedent, those were the laws he depended upon to assert his prerogative and mystery, that was the form of his entertainments, his Banqueting House, the ideology of his reign. John Chamberlain put the Roman comparison less kindly, but in a casual manner that suggests how pervasive it was. He wrote to Sir Dudley Carleton in 1614: "You may thincke there want no wooers for your place . . . when a knight whom you know well and whose name begins with R. Dru: would part with 2000[li] for the purchase, but yt were pitie things shold passe that way, for then we might well say *omnia Romae vaenalia*," in Rome everything is for sale. Comparisons of James with Tiberius were on the whole even less flattering.

The Roman plays that came to claim the stage in the Jacobean period reflect the style of the monarch and James's sense of himself as royal actor. They bear, as *romanitas* does in the Renaissance, a strong notion of public life, the continuities of history, the recreation of Rome as England's imperial ideal. In this Roman world, a particular kind of hero exists. In him, the absolutism that James espoused in his own self-division is tragically revealed. Absolute, measurable only by himself, he is described by himself. Cleopatra recognizes this in Antony: "none but Antony / Should conquer Antony" (4.15.16–17). Antony is—simply—Antony, even when he is not: "when he is not Antony / He comes too short of that great property / Which still should go with Antony" (1.1.57–59). And he is never more himself than when he plays that particular Roman's part that Brutus plays in his final scene, suicide. "A Roman, by a Roman / Valiantly vanquished" (4.15.57–58), Antony puts it. Absoluteness coincides with self-destruction: "There is left us / Ourselves to end ourselves" (4.14.21–22). Self-referentiality doubles back upon itself; the hero who is sui generis undoes himself. In the Roman heroes, the Jacobean stage offers the image of the tragedy implicit in the royal role of the actor replaying the spectral kingdom of Augustus on the stage of history. . . .

After the bloodletting in Pompey's Theater, the theater of cruelty gives way to the ritual act by which the death of Caesar is inscribed in history. The history of liberty turns out to be the history of dramatic performance:

> BRUTUS: Stoop, Romans, stoop,
> And let us bathe our hands in Caesar's blood
> Up to the elbows and besmear our swords.
> Then walk we forth, even to the market place,
> And waving our red weapons o'er our heads,
> Let's cry "Peace, freedom, and liberty!"
> CASSIUS: Stoop then and wash. How many ages hence
> Shall this our lofty scene be acted over
> In states unborn and accents yet unknown!
> BRUTUS: How many times shall Caesar bleed in sport,
> That now on Pompey's basis lies along
> No worthier than the dust!
> CASSIUS: So oft as that shall be,
> So often shall the knot of us be called
> The men that gave their country liberty.
>
> (3.1.105–8)

The "now" in this performance demands that it refer to the real event, not the staged one. Yet, in fact, the lines are about that performance, too, and the claims upon an audience that they can make. They can make us believe that the staged event is real. The "acting over," the representation before our eyes, may be taken for the act itself; and perhaps what the perfect reciprocity of the metaphor hints is that history itself may be a series of representations. The acts on the stage of history in Brutus's formulation embody power in a form of transcendent constancy; events recur but do not change, unique events are acted over. We could say that the shape of these lines conveys something of that meaning: two voices speak, the brotherly coconspirators Brutus and Cassius, two voices, and yet as one. Brutus's reiterated "stoop" is Cassius's first word, his initial "how many" echoed by Brutus; the passage demonstrates an "acting over" in its own cumulative repeating rhetorical patterns. There is one language here, although there are two voices. That language has many names. We might call it politics, or power, or theater, or impersonation, or action. Thomas Heywood provides a good gloss. Actors, he says, are such powerful impersonators that they can bewitch us into thinking "the Personater were the man Personated." That statement may carry a profound truth if all the world is a stage and all men are actors. And, as for Roman actors, Heywood says: "If wee present a forreigne History, the subject is so intended, that in the lives of *Romans, Grecians,* or others, either the vertues of our Countrymen are extolled, or their vices reproved." Reversing Horatio, we might say that Hamlet discovers that to act at all one must be more Roman than Dane, especially if one is to play the king. It is in the closet, after all, that Polonius, once again, enacts the part of Julius Caesar; he falls to an actor who, having avoided the role of Nero, has become Brutus instead.

Let us begin by seeing how Brutus comes to be an actor.

The extraordinary scene occurs barely one hundred lines into *Julius Caesar.* Caesar and his entourage have passed across the stage briefly as they pursue the course for the celebration of the Lupercal, leaving Cassius and Brutus behind. Throughout the subsequent scene which Brutus and Cassius play together, another will occur offstage, the offer of a crown to Caesar thrice refused and the final swoon in the marketplace when Caesar falls before the crowd. These offstage events punctuate those onstage; this is the only moment in all of Shakespeare when the backstage area is conceived of as one on which the action onstage depends, one continuous with action onstage. Normally, the *frons scenae* defines a limit, occasionally pierced by the opening of the discovery space. In the tiring house behind, costumes (attire) are changed, and the actor retires. But, in this scene in which Brutus emerges into public life, the very deployment of the stage carries a parallel structure. Public life is pervasive. There is no privacy, no retirement, no place to shift a scene or change a costume. Even behind the scenes, the actors continue to impersonate. The very shape of the stage serves, then, to carry a meaning we have seen before, the continuity of inner life and outer life, private and public. What the stage conveys, the scene portrays: Brutus is born as an actor in this scene, ushered into his part; he emerges as a public figure.

The scene between Brutus and Cassius begins with a piece of observation, "Brutus, I do observe you now of late" (1.2.32), that alerts us to the fact that there is no way *not* to be observed, no retiring from view. Cassius's observation here is knotty, complex. He complains that Brutus does not appear to love him, and Brutus responds with assurances that he does. Yet this very private matter is hardly all that they are talking about. The opportunity for Cassius's observation is, after all, the fact that Brutus has markedly absented himself from Caesar's retinue; perhaps Brutus has even provoked Cassius's observation by his sour remarks about Antony. "Will you see the order of the course?" (l. 25) was Cassius's first question to Brutus, and his refusal triggers Cassius's observation. The complaint about love, then, raises questions about taking sides; implicitly, Cassius questions where they stand in relation to Caesar—and Antony's "quick spirit" that Brutus confesses he lacks. (There are ironies in that confession: it is Antony who will run the race, it is upon Antony's touch that Caesar rests the hope of issue, and it is Antony who, in response to Caesar's commands, replies, "I shall remember. / When Caesar says 'Do this,' it is performed" [ll. 9–10]. Antony's role is to be the echo of Caesar, the fulfillment of his word, embodied in performance. Antony takes upon himself to extend himself to represent Caesar. Antony's performance becomes history, as firmly as Cassius's lack of love for plays marks out his destiny.)

Cassius and Brutus raise a "quick spirit" of performance, not around the presence of Caesar and his imperial word, but around his absence—of which we are always reminded by the shouts of the crowd breaking through the scene, each time heightening its

rhythms, lending urgency to the emergence of Brutus as conspirator—his absence, and Cassius's portrait of Caesar as no god but as
the most mortal of men. The absent Caesar and the image of his
diseased body, fallible, weak, frail: against these the conspiratorial,
quick-spirited scene onstage is played. The Caesar offstage dominates
what occurs onstage, a form of power we know James favored,
withdrawing from view and into his absolute state. And we know,
too, that state secrets sometimes masked the body. Here, Cassius's
tale, Caesar's swoon, are private realms beneath the claims to deity
and the crown offered—and, characteristically, denied—offstage.

Also backstage are correspondent segments of Brutus and Cassius, parts of themselves equally private, fallible and as unavailable
as the scene not seen. Offstage and on, a crown is being offered;
Caesar refuses it, yet Casca says his no means yes. Brutus will not
even quite acknowledge that Cassius has made the offer. The scene
will end in silence, just before Caesar returns from the Forum, Brutus
having emerged so far into public life that he will cover his emergence
with the very absences and denials that mark Caesar's performance
and thus suggest his attainment of power. He says to Cassius:

> That you do love me I am nothing jealous.
> What you would work me to, I have some aim.
> How I have thought of this, and of these times,
> I shall recount hereafter. For this present,
> I would not so (with love I might entreat you)
> Be any further moved. What you have said
> I will consider; what you have to say
> I will with patience hear, and find a time
> Both meet to hear and answer such high things.
> Till then, my noble friend, chew upon this:
> Brutus had rather be a villager
> Than to repute himself a son of Rome
> Under these hard conditions as this time
> Is like to lay upon us.
>
> (ll. 162–75)

The scene begun with a question of love ends with loving assurance.
Love now has some explicit consequences, as explicit as Caesar's
desire for issue, with which the scene opens, the imperious voice
stopping the procession to proclaim his wife's barrenness. The scene
is framed by this transformation of what might be thought of as the

most private and intimate into matters of public concern. Caesar's imperious command serves as a precedent for making privacy public, and Shakespeare's art in this scene is to open to observation what might have been thought to be unobservable—or unspeakable. Love is politics. In his love, Brutus would make time stop, although his speech keeps glimpsing a past and a future bound to this present. He would not be further moved and would move no further. Yet, his denials carry hints of revelations, hints of actions. Brutus, not saying what he has thought, or what he will do, admits that he has thought and that he will act; he defers his recounting to hereafter; he posits a time in the future meet for action and for speech. Deferring himself to then, he extends himself into the future. Note the progression of tenses: from the assurance of the present love through the conditionals and on to an insistent futurity of "I will . . . I will." The speech to Cassius ends with a prophecy, couched as prophecies are, gnomically; what exactly does Brutus promise? As he says, it needs to be chewed. These obscure words, hinting at rebellion, yet declaring (in opposition, unvoiced, to Antony) proper sonship, true filial piety to Rome, bring Brutus into the sphere of politics. This saying and not saying at once has put onstage what is yet offstage. Brutus has entered the second body in which power is invested, the invisible body of power.

Here is how it emerges:

Brutus says that what Cassius has observed reading his face—a lack of love—is something else, absorption in himself so that he has "veiled" his look (l. 37) forgetting "the shows of love to other men" (l. 47). Between the initial "If I have veiled my look" and the final acknowledgment of forgetfulness, Brutus disowns and owns the perception that Cassius has brought to his countenance. He has seen that Brutus is out of love. The question is, with whom: himself? Caesar? Brutus answers himself and Cassius reads it as out of love with Caesar. (Later in the play, Portia will wonder if Brutus no longer loves her, and she will be sacrificed to the ghost of Caesar, and to Brutus's transformation of himself into the man of marble constancy, unfeeling.) The veiled face may be veiled even to its owner. "Tell me, good Brutus, can you see your face?" (l. 51), Cassius asks; when Brutus admits that he can only see himself by reflection, Cassius offers (as Achilles does in *Troilus and Cressida*) to be the mirror in which Brutus may read himself. Cassius tells what Brutus believes hidden, what Brutus believes he hides in his self-absorption. Yet, plain to Cassius is what Brutus denies as "that which is not in me" (l. 65), which Cassius emends to "that of yourself which you yet know not of " (l. 70).

Brutus, self-absorbed, has retired into a private self, inarticulate, unrevealed, and unknown. To him, that self is nothing; "that which is not in me." Yet Cassius can read it in his face. To him it is public. This secreted self mirrors the offstage event, unacknowledged, denied. The hidden not-self that Brutus would deny is the public self clothed in the second body of power, a spiritual body, ghastly, ghostly, unchanging. Brutus, "with himself at war" (l. 46), is about to issue into a monstrous birth. Conspiring together, Cassius offering, as he reads Brutus's face, declarations of "my love" (l. 73), the not-self of Brutus is about to be acknowledged, to become the other self, conceptions "only proper to myself " (l. 41) reconceived. For at this moment, there is a flourish and a shout. "What means this shouting?" Brutus asks, and answers himself, becoming two voices at once. "I do fear the people / Choose Caesar for their king" (ll. 79–80).

The shout releases a fear, articulates "that which is not in me" (l. 65), explains the "veil" and the "show" of forgetfulness. Brutus has been denying what he has been thinking, denying the fear that breaks out of him as the crowd roars and shouts. And, suddenly, he makes a declaration, couched in those abstractions that will mark Brutus's speech throughout the remainder of the play—words that will be resounded over the corpse of Caesar.

> What is it that you would impart to me?
> If it be aught toward the general good,
> Set honor in one eye and death i'th'other,
> And I will look on both indifferently;
> For let the gods so speed me as I love
> The name of honor more than I fear death.
>
> (ll. 84–89)

Brutus reverses the direction of the scene; Cassius feeds him, does not draw him out. The coconspirators begin to identify, imparting— Cassius will call this seduction as the scene closes (l. 309). Imparting they join. And after the veiled looks, the tentative observation, the tortured reading in a mirror, Brutus finds what he can "look on . . . indifferently," a way of glossing himself that renames "that which is not in me" and calls it honor. Brutus is an honorable man—we know what will happen to the adjective he chooses to cover himself with, just as we know what to make of the cry of the conspirators, "Liberty! Freedom! Tyranny is dead!" (3.1.78). Every revolution has that rally. Without knowing it, with *honor* Brutus has arrived at the language of state, words housing contradictions that he will attempt to master and that will master him. The language of power, as James knew, cuts two ways. At this moment, Brutus chooses for himself *honor* and the *general good*. Cassius cements the connection between those names in the mirror he holds up for reflection: "I know that virtue to be in you, Brutus, / As well as I do know your outward favor" (ll. 90–91). Transparent Brutus, seen through: Cassius reverses his words.

Hence, "honor is the subject of my story" (l. 92) when Cassius proceeds to reveal that Caesar, the man that "is now become a god" (l. 116), bears a dying body that cannot command the flood and that shakes with fever. Observant Cassius has "marked" him, has seen his eye lose its luster, has heard him groan. Good physician, Cassius scorns his feeble temper. Against the Caesar of his "story" another "general shout" (l. 132) resounds, and Cassius is now ready to apply his tale of honor to the man of honor. He invites Brutus to substitute the names " 'Brutus' and 'Caesar.' What should be in that 'Caesar'? / Why should that name be sounded more than yours" (ll. 142–43). "Let him be Caesar" (3.2.50), the people will shout after Brutus has spoken over the corpse of Caesar. Cassius invites Brutus to compare the two names linked by honor, to weigh them, sound them, write them, conjure with them. He invites a double nomination and reminds Brutus of the history his name bears, for it is not his own but ancestral: "There was a Brutus once" (l. 159), he says, and there is a Brutus again. Brutus has two names, representing himself: Brutus and Caesar; Brutus in history—names to be inserted in a book, to be read, weighed, pondered. Brutus's word, self-chosen, leads him to his name, chosen for him: his career is already written, his name already inscribed. The duplicities of language find Brutus out, James's spectral history of inescapable repetition, a Roman view, is Brutus's, too.

Later, replaying the scene alone, reading in his garden, stones with words attached to them will be flung in, destroying his privacy, violating himself.

> The exhalations, whizzing in the air,
> Give so much light that I may read by them.

> "Brutus, thou sleep'st. Awake, and see thyself!
> Shall Rome, &c. Speak, strike, redress!"
> "Brutus, thou sleep'st. Awake!"
> Such instigations have been often dropped
> Where I have took them up.
> "Shall Rome, &c." Thus must I piece it out:
> Shall Rome stand under one man's awe? What, Rome?
> My ancestors did from the streets of Rome
> The Tarquin drive when he was called a king.
>
> (2.1.44–54)

Brutus "piece[s] out" the fragments and promises to act, binding himself to the example of his ancestors, acknowledging the not-self that Cassius gives him access to, the "hideous dream" that he shares with Calphurnia and that produces the savage spectacle of Caesar bleeding in Pompey's Theater:

> Since Cassius first did whet me against Caesar,
> I have not slept.
> Between the acting of a dreadful thing
> And the first motion, all the interim is
> Like a phantasma or a hideous dream.
>
> (2.1.61–65)

To Cassius's initial prompting, Brutus offers ambiguous promises, a prophetic riddle welcomed by Cassius as a "show" of something more (1.2.176). Another show follows immediately, Caesar's. For just as what was offstage in Brutus has come onstage in the concealed forms of political discourse, so Caesar returns. Now Brutus is all eye, knowing the force of observation: "But look you, Cassius, / The angry spot doth glow on Caesar's brow" (ll. 183–84). He has seen the need to observe, to read from the body to what it reveals. But despite all the signs of fear and anger, the blaze of eyes, the paleness of skin, all there before the eye, Caesar seems unfathomable. An interpreter is needed, and Casca will soon stay to tell. Caesar pauses to speak again, as he had done at first, to Antony; he speaks and unspeaks himself, talks of fear and fearlessness, of unchangingness, immovableness, "for always I am Caesar" (l. 212), and, in the same breath, of the weakness of his hearing. Observant, Caesar pauses over Cassius's looks, over his powers of observation: "He is a great observer, and he looks / Quite through the deeds of men" (ll. 202–3), and he closes by asking Antony to tell him what he thinks of Cassius. Nothing is revealed when two voices speak at once: Caesar's speech is the speech of power; there is more to him than can be observed.

And it is, according to Casca, with two voices that Caesar speaks. Each denial of the crown, he says, only showed how much he wanted it. Mere "foolery" is Casca's reiterated word for Caesar's show (ll. 235, 284), a performance as he reports it. "He put it by with the back of his hand thus" (l. 221), he gestures; claiming not to have "marked" the performance, Casca has observed all, seen through it. He can tell exactly what sort of crown it was, and how the breaths of the crowd stank, and the coup de théâtre when Caesar falls. Cassius tries to read the event symbolically; they, not Caesar, have the falling sickness, he tells Brutus; but Casca dismisses that allegorization for a more complex reading. He sees Caesar's swound as a theatrical event:

> If the rag-tag people did not clap him and hiss him, according as he pleased and displeased them, as they use to do the players in the theatre, I am no true man.
>
> (ll. 256–59)

Casca is no true man; once he has gone, Cassius will say that his blunt manner is something he "puts on" (l. 296), a piece of impersonation meant to add savor to his words. But, in Casca's account, Caesar is no true man either, but a consummate actor. Cassius had used a story about Caesar's infirm body as the theme of honor; Caesar uses his body itself to move the crowd. The body is transformed into an element of persuasion; it no longer bears a merely natural existence (did it ever?); through the body, we know, the royal actor is read. In the public forum, before the roaring crowd, Caesar transforms his dying body into the body of power:

> Marry, before he fell down, when he perceived the common herd was glad he refused the crown, he plucked me ope his doublet and offered them his throat to cut. An I had been a man of any occupation, if I would not have taken him at a word I would I might go to hell among the rogues. And so he fell. When he came to himself again, he said, if he had done or said anything amiss, he desired

their worships to think it was his infirmity. Three or four
wenches where I stood cried "Alas, good soul!" and for-
gave him with all their hearts. But there's no heed to be
taken of them. If Caesar had stabbed their mothers, they
would have done no less.

(ll. 261–72)

Between his infirm body and the crown he desires, Caesar constructs
a performance in which his body can be owned or disowned, in
which his deeds are countenanced and discountenanced, in which he
is present and absent in his actions and his words. Caesar's openness,
passion, honesty, and humility are all shows, yet not unreal, not
simply to be translated into something else as if they were an allegory,
or as if they were merely cynical. The language of state, we know,
is not simply a cover. The show that Caesar puts on manifests power.
"Well, Brutus, thou art noble," Cassius will say, alone, as the scene
closes, "yet I see . . ." (l. 305). "Thou art . . . ; yet." The syntax
here holds two truths together as the basis for political action and
political perception: two truths are essential to the imperial theme.
As the scene closes Cassius appears to have power, but, in fact, his
power is limited by his observations and his performance. He is never
again so consummate an actor; nor is Brutus. Rather, as the opening
of the scene suggested, the race belongs to Antony; his is the power
to ride the tide and issue forth.

Antony inherits the mantle of Caesar. He takes it and invests
that stage property with the savage spectacle. His function, he says,
alone with the corpse, is to put a mouth in the wounds, to make
them speak (3.2.229–30). Once again, the hidden and the private are
made public. With the crowd, the rent mantle of Caesar becomes
the prop for the representation of Caesar's death. He puts his words
in the holes of the mantle, and draws with them the blood of Caesar
and the rage of the crowd. When he removes the mantle, the veil,
he reveals the bleeding body, a body that has been clothed in the
words he has threaded through the mantle's holes. Caesar's body
becomes a prop behind the prop of the veil, and the veil serves as
the vehicle of discourse, a place in which Antony is invested and yet
not revealed, a place upon which the hidden springs of his action
and the actions of the crowd and the actions of the conspirators can
all be re-presented. The mantle is a figure for speech in the political
domain.

"You all do know this mantle" (3.2.170), Antony begins, but in fact, only he knows it. To it he attaches a memory, Caesar first wearing it one summer night when he secured Rome against one of its enemies. The rhythms here are casual, private, intimate; yet the very domesticity carries a political meaning. Thus the great man invested himself when he made the world safe for you; his leisure was only possible when he had first secured the general good.

> I remember
> The first time ever Caesar put it on.
> 'Twas on a summer's evening in his tent,
> That day he overcame the Nervii.
> (ll.170–73)

"Caesar put it on": *put on* is the Elizabethan idiom for playing a part, and Antony's account of it is, in the modern idiom, a "put on"; indeed we have no way of knowing what is true in this story despite all its sense of observation, the evening, the season, the day, the very gown. "I remember" is a pure reconstruction, a remembering indeed. And then, a dismembering.

> Look, in this place ran Cassius's dagger through.
> See what a rent the envious Casca made.
> Through this the well-beloved Brutus stabbed.
> (ll.174–76)

Look, says Antony, look at the holes. He constructs his story in those tears and rents. Through them he works, threading his words. Antony makes the daggers speak.

> And as he plucked his cursed steel away,
> Mark how the blood of Caesar followed it,
> As rushing out of doors to be resolved
> If Brutus so unkindly knocked or no.
> (ll.177–80)

The eye is invited to follow the invisible flow of blood, to enter an offstage area, the love of Brutus and Caesar violated, the bursting of a mighty heart, the mantling of his face in grief, falling beneath the bleeding statue of Pompey. The bleeding statue functions like the rent veil, for it, too, represents the double body of Caesar that falls and cannot die. This is the veil that Antony weaves, out of nothing, holes, wounds, a corpse. Over this body, he conjures that spectral one, to be seen, displayed, although it is invisible, the body of power, the king's spectral, spiritual body. "Look you here! / Here is himself, marred as you see with traitors" (ll. 196–97). Here is himself. Yet what is to be seen when we look is not the "bleeding piece of earth" (3.1.254) Antony saw when alone with the corpse. In public, another body is to be seen, the invisible body Antony invites the crowd to see, the ghost that Brutus finally sees. "Didst thou see anything," Brutus asks, and "Nothing, my lord" is the reply (4.3.297ff.). As Cassius confesses finally, before he plays "a Roman's part" (5.3.89), "My sight was ever thick" (l. 21).

> BRUTUS: Ha! who comes here?
> I think it is the weakness of mine eyes
> That shapes this monstrous apparition.
> It comes upon me. Art thou any thing?
> Art thou some god, some angel, or some devil,
> That mak'st my blood cold and my hair to stare?
> Speak to me what thou art.
> GHOST: Thy evil spirit, Brutus.
>
> (4.3.275–82)

So, finally, Brutus sees "that which is not in me" (1.2.65), the specter that haunts him as his double, invisible before his eyes, the spirit of Caesar mighty yet. At last, Brutus sees the very form of power before him.

Brutus's Nature and Shakespeare's Art

A. D. Nuttall

The eighteenth century was profoundly excited by the then novel
intuition that Shakespeare's works conveyed the nature of the real
world. This excitement lasted well through the nineteenth century
and still rises, unbidden, in the untheoretical reader, even today. But
in the twentieth century formalism came to Shakespeare criticism
before it appeared elsewhere. The origins of this formalism, indeed,
lie outside the twentieth century and outside England. Gustav Rü-
melin's *Shakespearestudien* (Stuttgart, 1866) is an important early essay
in this mode. The translation in 1922 of Levin Schücking's *Die Charakterprobleme bei Shakespeare* brought the new approach to the attention of the English-speaking world. The consequent critical
enterprise, powerfully led in the 1930s by E. E. Stoll, forms a distinct
movement, quite separate from structuralism, but sharing with
structuralism a hostility to the idea of mimetic veracity and a cor-
relative impulse to substitute codes and schemata for verisimilitude.
The identification of schemata was a positive gain. But the presumption that they must be treated as terminal objects of aesthetic
apprehension rather than as formulations of further meaning entailed
a very considerable loss. Stoll and others conceived their schemata
as necessarily intransitive. At an opposite pole, every ordinary
speaker of English treats the schemata of the English language as
transitive, as conducting the user to a reality which exists beyond
the linguistic forms. Similarly, ordinary theatregoers treat the very

From *A New Mimesis*. © 1983 by A. D. Nuttall. Methuen, 1983.

different stereotypes of drama as transitive, in so far as they pass through them into a world of probable inference.

L. C. Knights [in *Explorations*], following in the footsteps of Stoll, would have us understand that Falstaff "is not a man, but a choric commentary." In such statements the Opaque language of criticism rises up to condemn its former ally, the Transparent language. Knights's unguarded epigram expresses a hard formalist view and is as easily rebutted as such views always are. Falstaff is quite clearly presented, through fiction, as a human being. To strive to dislodge such fundamental and evident truths as this is a kind of critical idiocy. But the soft formalist position is a little more plausible. Falstaff Everyman and Jack the Giant Killer are all fictional people but they are not realistic. The emphasis in realistic art is on *possible* people, but in none of these cases is any strong interest shown in the area of possibility and probability, while, conversely, a great deal of interest is lavished on story, image, motif. They are therefore only minimally mimetic and such minimal mimesis does not invite or reward critical scrutiny. Once again the "weak thesis" is really the stronger one. Nevertheless, while they may be right about Jack and Everyman, they are wrong about Falstaff. The motifs and images are certainly there, but so is attentiveness to the world. The eighteenth-century critics were right. The poet of glorious, licentious imagination was also the poet of reverent and attentive perception. So long as we remember that fictions involve mediated truth to probabilities rather than immediate truth to specific facts, Shakespeare's plays may properly be seen as a continued feat of minute yet organized accuracy. So far in [*A New Mimesis*] the literary examples have been simple illustrations, appropriate—I hope—to some twist or turn of the argument. Shakespeare's imitation of the world, on the other hand, is a complex thing and we must take it slowly.

How Roman are the Roman plays of Shakespeare? Teachers of literature used confidently to assert that Shakespeare had no sense of anachronism. Clocks chime in *Julius Caesar* (2.1.192) and in *Coriolanus* the shortsighted wear spectacles (2.1.196). The notion that Shakespeare's Romans are really Elizabethans with specially sounding names persists. Students disparagingly observe that Shakespeare in *Antony and Cleopatra* betrays his complete ignorance of the most obvious and familiar of all Egyptian artefacts, the pyramids. In one sense they are quite right. The most ignorant student today probably has a better idea of the *appearance* of, say, a Roman senator or of the

Roman forum than Shakespeare had. The reason for this is simple. Schoolchildren now grow up with lavishly illustrated history books, with classroom walls liberally decorated with posters showing the Colosseum and the like. Shakespeare had none of these things. But he read certain ancient authors. So it comes about that, while he will blunder in the physical detail of daily life—that is, over things like clocks and spectacles—when he comes to deal with a Roman suicide, as distinct from an English suicide, he leaves the average modern student light-years behind. In the study of history Shakespeare lacked the means to walk, but he saw a way to run and seized it. The more sophisticated conceptions of later historians are easily within his reach.

For example, it is commonly believed that it takes a modern anthropologist or cultural historian to see that human nature may itself evolve in time. Previously history was a tract of battles, legislation and migration, all presumably conducted by persons fundamentally like ourselves. This was the doctrine from which C. S. Lewis at last prised away his mind in 1942, in his celebrated rejection of "the Unchanging Human Heart."

> How are these gulfs between the ages to be dealt with by the student of poetry? A method often recommended may be called the method of the Unchanging Human Heart. According to this method the things which separate one age from another are superficial. Just as, if we stripped the armour off a medieval knight or the lace off a Caroline courtier, we should find beneath them an anatomy identical with our own, so, it is held, if we strip off from Virgil his Roman imperialism, from Sidney his code of honour, from Lucretius his Epicurean philosophy, and from all who have it their religion, we shall find the Unchanging Human Heart, and on this we are to concentrate. I held this theory myself for many years, but I have now abandoned it. I continue, of course, to admit that if you remove from people the things that make them different, what is left must be the same, and that the Human Heart will certainly appear as Unchanging if you ignore its changes.

Could Shakespeare conceivably have discerned a change in the Human Heart, dividing the Romans from the people of his own time? Surely, it will be said, we can look for no glimmer of such a conception of human nature before, say, the novels of Sir Walter Scott; indeed, even tentatively to attribute such a conception to Shakespeare is historical solecism.

Yet Pope, who lived a hundred years before Sir Walter, saw some such thing in Shakespeare:

> In *Coriolanus* and *Julius Caesar*, not only the Spirit but Manners, of the *Romans* are exactly drawn; and still a nicer distinction is shown, between the manners of the *Romans* in the time of the former and of the latter.

It may be thought that Pope's emphasis on something as superficial as "manners" impairs my case. But by "manners" Pope intends far more than the formalized shibboleths of social intercourse. The Latin word for what he has in mind is mores. The modern English equivalent is likely to be polysyllabic and pseudotechnical: "sociocultural behaviour patterns." In any case, Pope has already taken it as read that Shakespeare captured "the spirit" of the Romans. But it is the extra discrimination proposed in the second part of his sentence that is especially challenging. Shakespeare did not merely distinguish Romans from English, he distinguished early Romans from later Romans.

Let us look first at Brutus, Cassius and Mark Antony, not as Romans, but less narrowly, as men having a culture which is, at least, different from ours, so that they may be conceived as belonging to an earlier phase in psychic evolution.

Brutus at once involves us in a large, though fairly standard question of cultural history. For Brutus, as is conceded on all hands, is obviously presented by Shakespeare as a conscious Stoic. Real-life Roman Stoicism is rather an aggregate of intellectual and social postures than the philosophy of a single, dominant thinker. Its common opposite, Epicureanism, is indeed derived from the teachings of one man, Epicurus, but few people can even name the master of the Stoics, Zeno. For the Elizabethans Seneca and, to a lesser extent, Plutarch and Virgil are the authoritative names. J. B. Leishman offers an admirable summary of the cult (I use the word in its modern, debased sense) in his book, *Translating Horace*:

> The central doctrine of Stoicism was that nothing mattered except virtue, that it was possible to detect in the world a divine purpose, guiding all things to their perfection, and

that it was man's duty to try to identify himself with this purpose, and to train himself to feel indifference towards everything else, except towards any possibility, whether public or private, of helping others to become virtuous. About Stoicism there was much metaphor, much striking of attitudes, much of what the Germans call *pathos*: life was a battle, in which the Stoic's soul remained unconquerable and his head, though bloody, unbowed; life was a play in which each man had been given a part which he was to read and act at sight and to the best of his ability, without knowing what might happen in the last scene; the Stoic ate and drank from gold as if it were clay and from clay as if it were gold; amid the ruins of a falling world he would but involve himself the more impenetrably in his *virtus*, and his soul would finally ascend through the spheres to a region beyond the sway of fortune.

Leishman catches admirably a certain duality which runs through Stoicism. There is, as he points out, much pathos about this philosophy of *apathia*, "emotionless tranquillity." The Stoics admired a condition of passionless indifference, but they also admired the heroic achievement of that condition. For the achievement to be spectacular or striking, some passion was after all required, if only as the material of moral conquest. Virgil's description, in book 4 of the *Aeneid*, of Aeneas shaken by Dido's plea that he stay with her, yet inwardly firm in his resolve, is one of the great images of Stoicism. Virgil likens his hero to a tree, tempest-torn yet firmly rooted, and ends his description with the famous, brief, enigmatic sentence:

> lacrimae volvuntur inanes.
>
> (the tears roll down in vain.)
>> (*Aeneid* 4.449)

The puzzle is: whose are the tears, Aeneas's or Dido's? Augustine, notoriously, thought the tears were Aeneas's (*City of God* 9.4). It is an interpretation entirely consonant with Stoicism: the suburbs of the personality rebel, but the virtuous will remains firm. Stoics are in one way like statues but it can be said with equal truth that the Stoic hero is typically wracked with strong emotions.

We must also notice that Stoicism is a "postphilosophical philosophy." Ancient philosophy falls roughly into two periods. The first (the only one which really deserves the name "philosophical") is the period of Socrates, Plato, Aristotle. It is characteristic of this period that thinkers should see themselves as lovers of wisdom, as seekers after or purveyors of truth, as people trying to find the right answers to the most difficult questions. In the second period a strange alteration comes over the philosophers: they now present themselves as purveyors of mental health. It is as if some immense failure of nerve, a kind of generalized neurosis, swept through the ancient world, so that the most serious thinkers found that their most urgent task was not to inform or enlighten but to heal. They begin indeed to sound like psychiatrists. This is the period of Stoicism and Epicureanism, in which the philosophers say, again and again, "Come to us and we will give you ἀταραξία," that is, *freedom from tumult, tranquillity*. The great Epicurean poet Lucretius sought to free his hearers from the crushing fear of death by arguing—somewhat surprisingly to modern ears—that death is total annihilation. The Romans of the first century B.C. were terrified of torture after death.

The Stoic commendation of apathia, "absence of feeling," is similar. Seneca wrote "consolatory epistles," to comfort people in distress (notice how it has now become natural to expect *solace* from a philosopher—very soon books will appear with such titles as *The Consolation of Philosophy*, which would have seemed strange to Aristotle). Writing to people broken by bereavement and similar misfortunes, the Roman Stoic recommends a kind of withdrawal from the world:

> Recipe te ad haec tranquilliora, tutiora, maiora.

> (Recollect yourself, back to these things which are more tranquil, safer, more important.)
>
> (Seneca, *Ad Paulinum: de brevitate vitae* 19.1)

Contempt of life (and, by implication, of all one's most demanding personal relationships) must be supplemented by a proper egoism; the mind is its own place, and, though a man be banished from his beloved country, yet he can always reflect that over his own mind he is undisputed king. Thus the rational man is a citizen of the world, true to himself, exempt from emotional commitment to particular people and places. He cannot be banished.

> Ideoque nec exulare unquam potest animus.

> (And so the mind can never suffer exile.)
>
> (Seneca, *Ad Helviam de consolatione* 11.7)

Animus quidem ipse sacer et aeternus est cui non possit inici manus.

(The soul itself is sacred and eternal and on it no hand can be laid.)

(Seneca, *Ad Helviam* 11.7)

When, however, it is rational to leave this worthless life, the philosopher does so, with a steady hand.

It is clear that Senecan Stoicism worked by a systematic introversion of psychic patterns surviving from a much older, heroic culture, something like the shame-culture analysed by E. R. Dodds in *The Greeks and the Irrational*. In a shame-culture no distinction is drawn between performing an action for the sake of glory and performing it out of virtue. Virtue itself is seen in strangely public terms, coinciding with elements which we think of as "merely external," like beauty and physical strength. The greatest literary monument of a shame-culture is the *Iliad* of Homer. But it is by no means confined to archaic Greece. Anthropologists have traced it in cultures as remote as that of eighteenth-century Japan. It is also vestigially present in our own culture. In Stoic philosophy the heroic ethic of pride, of glory in the sight of others, is cut off from its reliance on social esteem and made self-sufficient in each individual. The rational man is taught to fill the silence of his own skull with clamorous self-applause, with a majestically austere approbation of his own feats. Every man his own Achilles in his own, private Trojan War. Certain behavioural tricks of the old culture survive in Stoicism—the military strut, the strenuousness—but they have been strangely dehumanized. The vivid responsiveness of man to man has been deliberately dried up at its source and instead we seem to be watching a set of obscurely threatened statues. Truly for them, as Cicero said, *vita mors est*, "Life is a state of death."

All this, note, is about real Stoicism. How much of it is "noticed" in Shakespeare's Roman plays? I answer: pretty well all of it. Shakespeare knows that because Stoicism is an artificially framed philosophy, deliberately and consciously adopted by its adherents, any actual Stoic Roman will have within him un-Stoic elements. Your shame-culture hero Achilles, say, simply exemplifies that culture, but Stoicism is rather something at which you aim. The theory of shame-culture is posterior to and descriptive of the practice. The theory of Stoicism is prior to and prescriptive of practice. There are therefore elements of cultural tension present in Brutus which are absent from Achilles (and, one might add, from Othello, but more of that anon).

In the second scene of the first act of *Julius Caesar* Brutus is "sounded" by Cassius, as to his willingness to kill Caesar. Cassius brings to his task a profound knowledge of Brutus's personality. He begins with the basis of that personality, which is the inherited and very ancient notion of self as essentially that which is presented to others. Cassius says,

> Tell me, good Brutus, can you see your face?
> (1.2.51)

Brutus answers that the eye cannot see itself except by reflection, in some other object such as a mirror. Cassius swiftly offers himself as a reflector:

> I, your glass,
> Will modestly discover to yourself
> That of yourself which you yet know not of.
> (1.2.68–70)

Notice what is happening. Cassius is, in effect, teaching Brutus what to think. But he contrives to use an image which both apprises Brutus of the opinion of others (a powerful primitive incentive) and yet evokes the private, self-regarding virtue of the Stoics (since the heart of his challenge is, "Brutus, what do you think of yourself?"). All this is done with the image, carrying a simultaneous implication of self-absorption and external reference, of the glass. Such talk, we sense, is congenial to Brutus. Moreover the language of mirrors which Cassius uses to compass his end subtly apprises the audience that there may be something narcissistic in the Stoicism of Brutus. This note is struck again a little later when Brutus opens the letter in his orchard: "Brutus, thou sleep'st. Awake, and see thyself" (2.1.45).

But with all this Brutus is perhaps better than Cassius thinks him. In the orchard scene (2.1) we see his mind, not as it is when it is being manipulated by Cassius, but working alone, strenuously, struggling to determine what ought to be done:

> It must be by his death; and for my part,
> I know no personal cause to spurn at him,

But for the general: he would be crown'd.
How that might change his nature, there's the question.
It is the bright day that brings forth the adder,
And that craves wary walking. Crown him—that!
And then, I grant, we put a sting in him
That at his will he may do danger with.
Th' abuse of greatness is, when it disjoins
Remorse from power; and to speak truth of Caesar,
I have not known when his affections sway'd
More than his reason. But 'tis a common proof
That lowliness is young ambition's ladder,
Whereto the climber-upward turns his face;
But when he once attains the upmost round,
He then unto the ladder turns his back,
Looks in the clouds, scorning the base degrees
By which he did ascend. So Caesar may.
Then, lest he may, prevent. And since the quarrel
Will bear no colour for the thing he is,
Fashion it thus—that what he is, augmented,
Would run to these and these extremities;
And therefore think him as a serpent's egg,
Which, hatch'd, would as his kind grow mischievous,
And kill him in the shell.

(2.1.10–34)

Brutus sets out the case with scrupulous care. He knows nothing personally, here and now, against Caesar. The alpha and omega of the case against him is that he would like to be crowned King. That crowning might change a nature at present blameless. The case is not specific to Caesar, therefore. It is just that, commonly, when men are thus incongruously elevated, those who were not proud before become so. The case as Brutus puts it is tenuous and some critics have seen in this a sign that Brutus is feebly rationalizing a dark impulse which springs from the imperfectly repressed violence in him. In fact there are signs in the play of such a side to Brutus's nature, notably the strangely exultant "red weapons" (3.1.110), but I cannot think that the dominant tenor of this passage is mere rationalization. After all, rationalization usually aims at giving as powerful an appearance as possible of logical completeness. When Hamlet explains his sparing of Claudius at his prayers by observing that to kill a man in a state of grace would be to send him straight to heaven and hence would be no revenge (*Hamlet* 3.3.72–79), we have an argument at once watertight and insane, and there is therefore an excellent case for supposing that Hamlet is rationalizing his reluctance. Brutus is fairly close in conception to Hamlet, but the tone of this soliloquy, with "there's the question" in line 13, is closer to the beleaguered but still operative sanity of "To be or not to be" (*Hamlet* 3.1.56f.) than to the faceless logic of "Now might I do it, pat" (*Hamlet* 3.3.72). Brutus goes out of his way to stress the *tenuousness* of his case, pauses on all the weak links in the chain, and this, surely, is almost the opposite of rationalization.

I suspect that many who say that such a chain of reasoning is an inadequate basis for any major political act cannot have reflected how much political action is necessarily founded on exactly this sort of "lest he may, prevent" basis. I imagine that most people today would say that republicanism is better than despotism. If you ask them why, they are likely to say that it is right that a people should be, as far as possible, self-governing, rather than subjected to the will of a single individual. If you then point out that in any system which stops short of the total democracy of the (adult, male) ancient Athenians (we will set aside the rigidly aristocratic character of real Roman republicanism!) the processes of government are in fact carried out by representative officers and not by the people at all, the answer is likely to be that as long as the officers remain answerable to the people they are more *likely* to act in the interest of the people— and now, notice, we have begun to speak in terms of *probability*.

Now let us make the situation concrete. Imagine yourself a citizen of France, wondering whether to vote for someone rather like General de Gaulle: a figure at the height of his power, who has, let us say, shown a genius for getting his country out of a tight spot, for running a system in trouble. What would such voters say? Well, they would of course say many different things. But the ones who were worried by the idea of autocratic genius might well say, "The case against him is not personal; it's just that autocracy is inherently dangerous. Of course, we cannot predict with certainty that he will behave corruptly, it is just that he may, and because of that bare possibility it is our duty to stop him." The seemingly factual character of formally indicative sentences like "Autocracy is bad" resolves itself, in practice, into a cloud of (very serious) probabilities.

Assassination is, to be sure, somewhat more drastic than a transferred vote, but nevertheless Brutus's speech is both moving and impressive in its refusal to dress up a political rationale as something more watertight than it really is. It is curiously refreshing after reading the words of current politicians (who are under very great pressure to sound more certain than they can ever really be). The best place in Brutus's speech is the marvelously laconic

> So Ceasar may.
> Then, lest he may, prevent.
> (2.1.27–28)

The lines beginning "And since the quarrel / Will bear no colour for the thing he is, / Fashion it thus" (2.1.28–30) have also been misinterpreted. I used to think that this was an example of what may be called "dissociated motivation," the kind of thing which we shall see later in Iago, a man who *decides* what he will believe, what he will be moved by. This puzzled me, because it meant that, according to the scheme which was beginning to form in my mind, Brutus would have to be classified as "overevolved."

The underevolved archaic man includes in his ego many things we consider external. The ordinarily evolved man includes within the ego such things as feelings and beliefs but excludes physical attributes, to a greater or lesser extent. According to this sequence the overevolved man might narrow the field of the ego still further, until it was able to watch, in arrogant isolation, the inept dance of emotions and appetites, now psychically objectified. But I was wrong. Although there is a faint pre-echo of Iago here, this sentence has a different context and a different logic.

Brutus is not, in fact, proposing to feign a belief and then to execute the fiction in real life. He is saying to himself "It is no use trying to construct this case with reference to what I know of Caesar, now. Rather, put it this way." To paraphrase thus is indeed to soften the worrying word "fashion," which obstinately retains a suggestion of fiction (I have conceded a faint anticipation of Iago's *manner*). Nevertheless, the main tenor of the idiom is donnishly abstract rather than cynically self-manipulative. It is much closer to the philosopher's "Let's try the argument this way" than to "This shall be my motive." If it is asked, "Why, then, granting that the Iago-subaudition is only a subaudition, did Shakespeare allow it into the line?" the answer is, perhaps, because he wished to hint that the second state of mind was, in a sinister fashion, latent in the first; that the proper corruption of moral abstraction is diabolical cynicism. Brutus stands on the edge of a pit, but he has not yet fallen.

Moreover this psychic isolation of the reflective ego is not natural to Brutus as it is to Iago. It is really the product of a special moral effort, the Stoic assertion of reason against disabling emotion. For the beginning of "overevolved" dissociation of the ego from ordinary feeling is likewise latent, or present as a potential corruption, in Stoic philosophy. Aeneas, weeping yet successfully separating his reason from his love of Dido, is great and at the same time rather weird. The panic-stricken retreat into a private area of the mind as being alone governable by the rational will can lead, almost by its own inner impetus, to forms of scepticism which would have shocked the Stoics themselves. The person who is broken-hearted is given the dangerous consolation (dangerous, because it can in the long run erode the very notion of value) "You yourself can decide what is good and what is bad." Hamlet's "There is nothing either good or bad, but thinking makes it so" (2.2.248) is pivotal. It reaches back into Stoicism and forward into abysses of modern scepticism. But the contraction of the ego is the principal point at issue, and it is important to remember that in Stoicism this contraction always takes place in a context of moral effort. There is therefore a real difference between Brutus's straining to bring to bear reason, and reason alone, on the one hand and Iago's unblinking survey of his own motives on the other. Nevertheless there is in *Julius Caesar* a real, though faint, analogue to Iago, and that is Mark Antony.

Consider the behaviour of Mark Antony, first, when he moves into the circle of the assassins as they stand round the body of the newly slain Caesar (3.1) and, second, in his great oration (3.2). In 3.1, Antony moves, with great circumspection but also with extraordinary "nerve" within sword's length of men who may at any moment turn on him. He is their greatest potential danger, but the potentiality (as with Caesar) is fraught with doubt. These are the reasonings of a Brutus and it is on them that Antony counts. The conscientiousness of Brutus is for him a weakness to be exploited. Antony knows just how much of his grief for Caesar it is safe to express. He shakes hands with the murderers and is left alone on the stage, to plot the ruin of Rome.

Notice, in passing, that my entire account of this scene has been written in bull-bloodedly Transparent language; I have been considering Shakespeare's Brutus and Antony, not indeed as direct portraits of their historical originals, but at least as possible human beings and I have not scrupled to make inferences and even, at times, to guess. Yet, in the closing sentence of the last paragraph, I wrote, not "left alone in the Capitol," but "left alone on the stage." The logical slippage from the tenor to vehicle is entirely easy and creates no difficulties for the reader, because it mirrors a movement of the mind which is habitual to playgoers and playreaders.

We may further ask, is Antony sincere? The question, oddly enough, can be answered with slightly more confidence when the reference is to a fictional person (where the clues are finite) than with reference to a real-life person (where they are indefinite and in any case liable to subversion). I think that Antony is sincere. He feels real grief for Caesar but is, so to speak, effortlessly separate from the grief even while he feels it. We therefore have something which is psychologically more disquieting than the ordinary machiavel, who pretends emotion while he coldly intrigues for power. Antony feels his emotions and then *rides* them, controls them, moderating their force as need arises.

Thus the great oration is at once artificial and an authentically passional performance. I would have the actor, if he can, go so far as to weep in the delivery of it ("his eyes are red as fire with weeping"—3.2.115) in order to give maximum effect to the conclusion of the oration, at which point Antony, his own emotion ebbing from its licensed height, watches the mob run screaming from him and says, like one who has administered a mass injection, "Now let it work. Mischief, thou art afoot" (3.3.261). Naturally it is Brutus who is the man of the past, the doomed order of things, and Antony who is the man of the future. When Brutus patiently explained, with lucid logic, how he had killed his friend to save Rome from the rule of an individual, the crowd applauds him with the dreadful "Let him be Caesar" (3.2.50). They do not understand the rigorous, tormented morality of his action and he, in his turn, does not understand the place in history to which he has come.

The Romanness, the unEnglishness, of all this is evident. Moreover, within that powerfully imagined Romanness we have, not only contrasts of individual with individual, but prior contrasts, operating in the region intermediate between individuals and the cultural remoteness of Rome. I mean a contrast between different degrees of psychic and political evolution within a Roman setting. Brutus, the Republican, addresses a populace which spontaneously embraces monarchy, thus exemplifying one of the paradoxes of liberalism identified by Sir Karl Popper (though Plato was there before him): what happens when a democracy decides in favour of tyranny? Brutus, the aristocrat, his theoretic Stoicism borne on a foundation of shame-culture, on ancient heroic dignity, belongs to the Roman past. He can do the Stoic trick (rather like "isolating" a muscle) of separating his reason from his passions but he cannot exploit his own motivating passions with the coolness of an Antony. With all his fondness for statuesque postures Brutus remains morally more spontaneous than Antony.

In 4.3 there is a notorious textual crux. Brutus and Cassius quarrel and are uneasily reconciled. Shakespeare presents the quarrel with great realism and elicits from his audience a high degree of sympathy with both figures. At 4.3.141 Cassius observes, wonderingly, "I did not think you could have been so angry," and, a moment later, with a hint of a taunt so that we fear the quarrel may break out again, he adds,

> Of your philosophy you make no use,
> If you give place to accidental evils.
> (4.3.143–44)

Brutus answers, bleakly, that Portia, his wife, is dead. Cassius is at once overwhelmed with contrition at his own coarse hostility. Brutus tells, shortly, the horrible story of Portia's suicide by swallowing fire and calls for wine, to "bury all unkindness" (4.3.152). Titinius and Messala then enter. Brutus welcomes them, volubly, and the talk is all of military movements and public events in Rome. Then the spate of talk dries up and the following dialogue takes place:

MESSALA: Had you your letters from your wife, lord?
BRUTUS: No, Messala.
MESSALA: Nor nothing in your letters writ of her?
BRUTUS: Nothing, Messala.
MESSALA: That, methinks, is strange.
BRUTUS: Why ask you? Hear you aught of her in yours?
MESSALA: No, my lord.
BRUTUS: Now, as you are a Roman, tell me true.

MESSALA: Then like a Roman bear the truth I tell:
  For certain she is dead, and by strange manner.
BRUTUS: Why, farewell, Portia. We must die, Messala.
  With meditating that she must die once,
  I have the patience to endure it now.
MESSALA: Even so great men great losses should endure.
CASSIUS: I have as much of this in art as you,
  But yet my nature could not bear it so.

(4.3.179–93)

Brutus receives the news from Messala as if for the first time, although he has just confided to Cassius that he knows, and Cassius is still there, listening to every word. To make matters worse, Brutus's self-control is applauded as a Stoic feat and Brutus accepts the applause. And still Cassius is there, watching and listening.

The easiest way out of these difficulties is to suppose that Shakespeare wrote two alternative versions and that both have somehow survived, in incongruous juxtaposition, in the 1632 Folio text (the sole authority for this play). To take this course at one stroke removes both the difficulties and the tense excitement of the scene. Brents Stirling, in an article which may serve as a model of the proper marriage of literary criticism and textual scholarship, argued for the retention of both versions. He observes that Brutus is in a state of nervous excitement after the quarrel with Cassius (notice his extreme irritation with the sententious poet who enters at 4.3.122). In this state, bordering on exhaustion, Brutus attempts to put Messala aside with his blankly mendacious "Nothing" at line 182. But Messala will not be put off and Brutus is forced to question him. Thereupon *Messala* "turns witless in the crisis" and answers "No, my lord" at 184. Brutus tries to resolve the impossible situation with "Now, as you are a Roman, tell me true." Messala catches the manner, is freed from his petrified immobility by the familiar *style*, and from here on forces Brutus to play out the episode in the full Stoic manner. At its conclusion Brutus's head is bowed at the humiliating praise he has received from Messala.

Given this reading, the comment of Cassius is immediately luminous. He has watched his fellow commander, in a state of near-collapse, lie and then reassert, artificially, his command over himself and his subordinates. Brutus's "Nothing" was pure nature. It is the kind of speech which in life is wholly probable and becomes "impossible" only when challenged by the customary canons of art.

Brutus then pulled himself back and this too was nature. From the recovered ground he framed his formal response to Messala and secured the required result. Cassius who has seen the "nature" of Brutus humiliated in the lie also perceives in the very recovery of will a feat of natural endurance. His comment is almost ironic but is at the same time movingly generous and intelligent; he observes that he could just about match Brutus's rhetoric, but he could never be so strong and brave.

This is not to say that there are no rough edges in the text as we have it. There is formal evidence in the Folio of revision. This has been investigated by Brents Stirling in a second article. The speech headings give "Cassi" until "Enter a Poet." Then, in the lines which report the death of Portia we get "Cas." At line 164, "Portia, art thou gone?" (which may be a single-line insertion), we get "Cass." The passage containing suspected additions has different prefix forms and the passages both before and after it have standard forms. Admittedly there is considerable variation of "Cassi" and "Cas" throughout the play and this must weaken the presumption of interpolation in so far as it is founded on speech headings. But the changes are so timed (in conjunction with the obvious oddity of the presentation) as to suggest some sort of process of revision, which has not been satisfactorily completed. What is not shown at all is that the revision was intended as a replacement of one version by another. It remains entirely possible that Shakespeare, revising, determined to show us a Brutus reacting twice to the same event and merely failed to complete the "joinery." Brutus's lie might then have been more carefully "framed." We need not infer that it would have been removed.

Thus, even when Brutus's Stoicism is most artificial, most plainly exerted by will, we sense not only what is exerted but the human will which exerts; we sense a person with an emotional life. That indeed is why the artificiality is so excruciating. In Antony it would scarcely be noticed.

Brutus is presented by Shakespeare as an interplay of nature and art; the art, to be sure, is Brutus's. If we step back and view the whole, both the art and the nature of Brutus are equally formed by the art of Shakespeare. Brutus's nature is Shakespeare's art. But in conveying something which the audience will receive as nature, Shakespeare must (and does) consult and defer to reality. Therefore among the many excellencies of *Julius Caesar* we may include a specific success in realism.

Ironic Heroism in *Julius Caesar:*
A Repudiation of the Past

James C. Bulman

The idioms Shakespeare employed to delineate heroism in his early plays were too restrictive to allow him a personal signature. It is not by chance that these plays for years were thought to be the work, or at least to contain the work, of other dramatists: they fully partake of the conventions that were the stock-in-trade of stage heroism. But together they constitute only Shakespeare's apprenticeship to already-established writers. Within a few years, he was forging a mimesis more sophisticated than any that had yet been tried and, as a consequence, was recutting the heroic patterns that only yesterday he had found fashionable enough. His new heroes were characterized by their awareness of conventional expectations, and their tragedies arose from their failure to live up to them—from their inability to wear hand-me-down roles with any comfort or conviction. The authenticity of the plays themselves sprang likewise from their simultaneous employment and repudiation of the conventions that had bodied forth a heroic reality in the "old plays."

The death of Caesar illustrates how Shakespeare had come to use conventions with detachment, even irony. *Julius Caesar* is often labeled a sort of revenge play, harking back to various Senecan plays on the theme of Caesar's hubris and perhaps directly to an academic play called *Caesar's Revenge*. Certainly it has the ethical confrontations and at times the rhetorical style of Senecan offshoots; and the

From *The Heroic Idiom of Shakespearean Tragedy.* © 1985 by Associated University Presses, Inc. University of Delaware Press, 1985.

trappings of portentous storms, daggers, ritual murder, and a vengeful ghost cast it in the mold of the more popular *Spanish Tragedie* and *Locrine*. Caesar himself bestrides the stage like a conquering colossus. He has an egotistical self-assurance to rival Tamburlaine's—"for always I am Caesar" (1.2.212)—and an imperious will that bends to no external persuasion—"The cause is in my will. I will not come" (2.2.71). His epic hubris, the insolent pride that dares fate to match him in a test of strength, finds apt expression in the conventional outdoing topos:

> Danger knows full well
> That Caesar is more dangerous than he.
> We are two lions litter'd in one day,
> And I the elder and more terrible.
>
> (2.2.44–47)

And his passionate assertion of heroic selfhood is supremely embodied in the rhetorical set-piece he delivers just prior to his murder. The epic simile, with enough Ovidian fire to make the gods blush, is strongly reminiscent of Tamburlaine:

> I am constant as the northern star,
> Of whose true-fix'd and resting quality
> There is no fellow in the firmament.
> The skies are painted with unnumb'red sparks,
> They are all fire and every one doth shine,
> But there's but one in all doth hold his place.
> So in the world: 'tis furnish'd well with men,
> And men are flesh and blood, and apprehensive;
> Yet in the number I do know but one
> That unassailable holds on his rank,
> Unshak'd of motion. And . . . I am he.
>
> (3.1.60–70)

With the hyperbole that has characterized all conqueror heroes, Caesar ingenuously identifies in himself an absolute integrity of self and self-image. Like Talbot, he is what he says he is—a godlike hero of mythic proportions. The language defines him as such; and public acclaim, heard offstage each time he refuses the crown, affirms it. But Shakespeare does not let this assertion stand unchallenged. Against that offstage acclaim, he gives us an antiphonal voice *onstage* that relentlessly, right up to the time of the murder, points out Caesar's naked frailties: he is deaf in one ear; he has epilepsy; Cassius once had to save him from drowning. Even his wife Calpurnia qualifies our admiration by gently mocking his vaunt as unwise boasting: "Alas, my lord, / Your wisdom is consum'd in confidence" (2.2.48–49). In the judgment of various Renaissance historians, such hubris provided ample justification for Caesar's murder; and so Brutus characterizes it: "People and senators, be not affrighted. / Fly not; stand still. *Ambition's debt is paid*" (3.1.82–83, my italics).

But much as Brutus would like to conceive of Caesar's death as a moral exemplum, a just retribution in the tradition of the *Fall of Princes,* he cannot: he is too circumspect to believe in the public construction he puts on it. Like a chivalric defender of national honor in the early histories, or even more like Titus who takes great risks to preserve Rome's honor, Brutus would define his role in Caesar's death as that of heroic justicer. He would prefer to regard the murder as consonant with public rather than private honor—

> If it be aught toward the general good,
> Set honor in one eye and death i' th' other,
> And I will look on both indifferently;
>
> (1.2.85–87)

—but he senses more deeply that his role likens him to a revenger who calls wrongs to a private accounting without recourse to law.

Brutus is aware that he has insufficient evidence of those "wrongs" to justify the murder. "To speak truth of Caesar, / I have not known when his affections sway'd / More than his reason" (2.1.19–21). Thus, in order to persuade himself, he must conjecture some future cause and proceed to act on that conjecture as if it were proof:

> And, since the quarrel
> Will bear no color for the thing he is,
> Fashion it thus.
>
> (2.1.28–30)

The vocabulary of his internal debate, "Fashion it thus," reveals in him an active will to dissemble. He will seek no "cavern" to mask the "monstrous visage" of conspiracy, but rather will "hide it in smiles and affability" (ll. 80–82, passim). Beyond the mask of smiles, he advocates a grander imposture that would disguise blood revenge in the cloak of ceremony. "Let's be sacrificers, but not butchers," he urges his fellow conspirators (l. 166):

> And let our hearts, as subtle masters do,
> Stir up their servants to an act of rage,
> And after seem to chide 'em. This shall make
> Our purpose necessary, and not envious;
> Which so appearing to the common eyes,
> We shall be call'd purgers, not murderers.
>
> (2.1.175–80)

Brutus's advice to his coconspirators is remarkably like Volumnia's to Coriolanus: as the public eye alone will determine the legitimacy of your heroic fame, act the part nobly, even if you do not believe in it. The pretense to heroism, reflected in the "seem" and the "so appearing," is ironic because Brutus would include his own among the "common eyes" he is trying to deceive. With a duplicity of which the more conventionally drawn heroes of Shakespeare's earlier plays were incapable, Brutus teaches his fellows to play a role to convince the audience of their integrity, and at the same time he would convince himself that the role is perfectly consistent with his ethical selfhood. He would be as absolute as Caesar in believing himself a hero. The traditional heroic vocabulary he uses conveys that wish: "our hearts," seats of the will, must stir "their servants," the passions, to "an act of rage," an essential component of heroes from Achilles onward. And why? Because murder resulting from a noble wrath will always be condoned as a heroic deed. So strong is Brutus's wish, in fact, that it almost fathers self-delusion.

His wish is undermined by the self-consciousness with which he uses the heroic idiom, however. In his attempt to use the idiom to effect only an *appearance* of heroic purpose, its credibility as a means of representing reality suffers. Brutus tries hard to convince us otherwise. To reinforce the legitimacy of his purpose, he resorts to a form of traditional oath-taking; but he metamorphoses it into a fellowship of honesty, suggesting that the reality of the oath transcends mere words: "What need we any spur but our own cause. . . . And what other oath / Than honesty to honesty engag'd?" (ll. 123, 126–27). Shakespeare recalls for us the moment when the Andronici, with no discrepancy between a heroic sign and its significance, took vows against Saturninus, and the even earlier episode when York's family vowed revenge against Clifford. Brutus adopts the ritual—

"Give me your hands all over, one by one" (l. 112)—only to try to outdo it in high-minded pretense: "No, not an oath. If not the face of men, / The sufferance of our souls, the time's abuse" (ll. 114–15). But in declining the oath itself, in reaching instead for something more universal, he fails to engage himself with the form and with the power of its accumulated meaning that generations of heroes had counted on for sustenance. The self-consciousness with which he manipulates the form betrays his detachment from the ethos it signifies.

Brutus's failure to be engaged with the forms he enacts is dramatized even more explicitly in the murder of Caesar. Ritual murder scenes were a popular part of the revenge tradition. Shakespeare had played them to the hilt in his *Henry VI* plays, especially when Edward, Richard, and Clarence one by one stab young Prince Edward before his mother's eyes (*3 Henry VI* 5.5) and again, even more sensationally, in the Thyestian banquet of blood that concludes the festivities in *Titus Andronicus*. Caesar himself had been ritually murdered in the academic *Caesar's Revenge,* falling to the music of Cassius's couplet, "Stab on, stab on, thus should your Poniards play, / Aloud deepe note upon this trembling Kay" (ll. 1699–1700), and confronted at the last by Brutus's stern rebuke:

> But lives hee still, yet doth the Tyrant breath?
> Chalinging Heavens with his blasphemies,
>
> . . . .
>
> I bloody *Caesar, Caesar, Brutus* too,
> Doth geeve thee this, and this to quite *Romes* wrongs.
>
> (ll. 1723–24, 1729–30)

Shakespeare's Brutus, unlike his earlier counterpart, is not content simply to do the deed out of moral conviction. Rather, he arranges Caesar's murder as a theatrical event. He directs his accomplices to play their parts "as our Roman actors do, / With untir'd spirits and formal constancy" (2.1.226–27)—an admission that constancy is no more to him than outward form—and bestows legitimacy on the murder by bidding them to bathe their hands in Caesar's blood, besmear their swords, then walk with him to the market-place,

> And, waving our red weapons o'er our heads,
> Let's all cry, "Peace, freedom, and liberty!"
>
> (3.1.109–10)

Through these conventional signs of ritual sacrifice, Brutus hopes to persuade his audience of Romans that Caesar's murder was a heroic act—a purge of tyranny, as in the old play—and that he and his accomplices are liberators, Rome's saviors, not butchers. He and Cassius even speculate that players in "ages hence" will reenact this "lofty scene" to the glory of their memory. "How many times shall Caesar bleed in sport," Brutus ponders (l. 114); and in so pondering, he "places" the event in a theatrical context and attempts to convince us, as well as himself, that outward shows may *create* a substantial reality.

Allusion to the theater was not new to a Shakespearean hero. As far back as *3 Henry VI,* Warwick, in his scene of oath-taking, had asked in agitation,

> Why stand we like soft-hearted women here,
> Wailing our losses, whiles the foe doth rage,
> And look upon, as if the tragedy
> Were play'd in jest by counterfeiting actors?
> (2.3.25–28)

Warwick's rejection of jest and counterfeit, however, affirms the reality of himself, his friends, and their cause: they must not act, but *be,* revengers. Brutus's use of theatrical imagery is far more complex. He tries to make acting and being inseparable. He instructs his friends to counterfeit like actors; he embraces the ritual shows by which he will win public approval; he conceives of the murder throughout as a scene played for posterity. Reality, for him, may be no deeper than the stage. But if the audience sees that Brutus can manipulate conventions to give a false appearance of heroism, then one's faith in conventional criteria for judging the reality of heroism on the stage cannot rest secure. The nature of dramatic illusion shifts. We do not trust, as Brutus hopes the Romans will trust, in the absolute correspondence of sign and significance. We may see more heroism in Brutus's struggle to come to terms with the heroic idiom than we see in the idiom itself. His self-consciousness becomes more compelling than his actual deeds. And the tension he feels between aping heroic forms and knowing that those forms are, for him, counterfeit, *makes* him real in a way that no conventionally drawn hero, not even Caesar himself, could ever be.

Shakespeare treats the heroic idiom with more irony in the various voices Antony adopts following Caesar's death. Most famous

of these is the voice of heroic revenger. Left alone, after the conspirators have departed, Antony addresses Caesar's corpse in a lament
that harks back to Clifford's lament over the corpse of his father, in
which he vows to dry up all tears of pity in a "flaming wrath" and
to find solace in cruelty. But Antony's prophecy is more universal:

> A curse shall light upon the limbs of men;
> Domestic fury and fierce civil strife
> Shall cumber all the parts of Italy;
> Blood and destruction shall be so in use
> And dreadful objects so familiar
> That mothers shall but smile when they behold
> Their infants quartered with the hands of war,
> All pity chok'd with custom of fell deeds.
>
> (3.1.263–70)

It stems from a long tradition of curse and threat of the sort that
Shakespeare sprinkled liberally through his histories. Tamburlaine
had called on it, "threatening a death and famine to this land," at
the death of Zenocrate. Talbot had threatened to "conquer, sack,
and utterly consume" Bordeaux; and Henry V, to shut up the gates
of mercy and mow "like grass" the "fresh-fair virgins" and "flow'r-
ing infants" of Harfleur. Behind these manifestations lie imprecations
in earlier English tragedies that invoke both biblical sources, such as
this in *Gorboduc:* "But dearth and famine shall possesse the land! /
The townes shall be consumed and burnt with fire"; and classical
sources, such as this in *Jocasta:* "And angry *Mars* shall ouercome it
all / With famine, flame, rape, murther, dole and death." But Antony
does not forget the more Senecan elements of revenge tragedy either.
The ghost that appeared three times in *Caesar's Revenge,* once in the
company of Discord, who comes from hell to ring down civil war,
may be on his mind when he says,

> And Caesar's spirit, ranging for revenge,
> With Ate by his side come hot from hell,
> Shall in these confines with a monarch's voice
> Cry "Havoc!" and let slip the dogs of war.
>
> (3.1.271–74)

Antony's speech thus fuses rhetorical traditions with remarkable
originality by sounding the voices of prophecy, curse, and threat all
at once. Ironically, the warning of impending horrors, usually spoken

by a choric observer such as Carlisle who, in *Richard II,* prophesies another Golgotha, here is spoken by the man who will bring those horrors about. The prophecy is thus self-fulfilling: not Caesar's spirit, but Antony himself, will let slip the dogs of war. Antony's language, on reflection, seems to be spoken with a self-conscious passion; and one may grow more suspicious that he is employing the heroic idiom to disguise his motives when, in the Forum scene that immediately follows, he turns revenge to political advantage and manipulates the throng with rhetorical artifice. His method is well known, so I shall cite just one overlooked allusion to revenge tradition to prove my point. Claiming that he is not disposed to "stir" the "hearts and minds" of the people "to mutiny and rage" against the "honorable men" who killed Caesar (3.2.123–26)—a disclaimer that echoes the language Brutus uses to stir the conspirators to do the deed—Antony produces Caesar's will, which, he says, "I do not mean to read":

> Let but the commons hear this testament—
> . . . .
> And they would go and kiss dead Caesar's wounds
> And dip their napkins in his sacred blood.
>
> (3.2.132–35)

Antony's lines poignantly recall the by-then-famous scenes in which Hieronimo dipped his napkin in Horatio's blood as a token of revenge and in which Margaret tormented York with the napkin dipped in the blood of his son Rutland. It is important to recognize the power of Antony's allusion. He says, in effect, that if the people knew the will of Caesar, they would all turn into Hieronimos ranging for revenge against the "honorable" assassins. He adopts, for the moment, a diction that had served him in his earlier lament and to which, after this, he need not return. The arch control of his Forum speech, in fact, employs little of such emotive language. He has no need for it. The allusion to *The Spanish Tragedie* simply is a reminder of an idiom Antony had milked and then cast off. In his shift of rhetorical gears, Shakespeare marks Antony's emergence from the role of antique revenger to the role of Machiavellian leader who recognizes, like the later Ulysses and Aufidius, that virtue lies in the interpretation of the times.

Antony's manipulation of the revenge idiom should not come as a revelation in the Forum scene. Even before his lament, he tries out different voices that serve his immediate purposes. Entering

the conspirators, uncertain of what they have in store for him, he at
once adopts the conventional language of *de casibus* tragedy, moralizing in best *ubi sunt* tradition the ephemeral nature of man's
greatness:

> O mighty Caesar! Dost thou lie so low?
> Are all thy conquests, glories, triumphs, spoils,
> Shrunk to this little measure? Fare thee well.
>
> (3.1.149–51)

In this are the seeds of Hamlet's "Imperious Caesar, dead and turn'd
to clay, / Might stop a hold to keep the wind away" (5.1.213–14).
But Antony is canny. Recognizing that Brutus will most respect a
noble response to the murder of a friend, Antony turns to the lurid
vocabulary of blood tragedy to *dare* the conspirators to butcher him
too:

> I do beseech ye, if you bear me hard,
> Now, whilst your purpled hands do reek and smoke,
> Fulfill your pleasure.
>
> (3.1.158–60)

The dare works: it forces Brutus to defend his deed against Antony's
characterization of it as a crime and, in the process, to offer Antony
an honorable love. Antony seizes the opportunity to insure his safety
by ceremonially shaking hands with the conspirators—

> Let each man render me his bloody hand.
> First, Marcus Brutus, will I shake with you;
> Next, Caius Cassius, do I take your hand;
> Now, Decius Brutus, yours; now yours, Metellus;
>
> (3.1.185–88)

—and adopts thereby a traditional heroic form that Brutus had tried
to surpass in claiming that inner honesty, not outward show, determined the honor of his course. Outward show stands Antony in
good stead here.

Yet he fears that his credit may stand on slippery ground. By
too easily embracing a heroic alliance with the enemies of Caesar,
he thinks they may have cause to suspect his honesty. Cunningly,
he puts the question to them: "what shall I say?" (l. 191). What he
decides to say is politically shrewd: first, to beg Caesar's forgiveness

for his apparent betrayal, then to lapse back into lament for greatness gone:

> Pardon me, Julius! Here wast thou bay'd, brave hart,
> Here didst thou fall, and here thy hunters stand,
> Sign'd in thy spoil, and crimson'd in thy lethe.
> O world, thou wast the forest to this hart,
> And this, indeed, O world, the heart of thee!
> How like a deer, strucken by many princes,
> Dost thou here lie!
>
> (3.1.205–11)

To the conspirators, this sounds convincing enough to be interrupted. To us, it ought to sound like "art." The style—one Antony has not used before—is Ovidian. The pun on "heart" anticipates that of Orsino who, some one or two years later, laments that he is another Acteon hounded by his desires: this romantic context tells us something about the artifice of such verse. But Antony's pretty conceit about the hunted hart bears a more striking resemblance to Shakespeare's early narrative poetry and to the pastoral similes and crimson conceits by which Titus and Marcus prettified Lavinia's mutilation:

> MARCUS: O, thus I found her, straying in the park,
> Seeking to hide herself, as doth the deer
> That hath receiv'd some unrecuring wound.
> TITUS: It was my deer, and he that wounded her
> Hath hurt me more than had he kill'd me dead.
>
> (3.1.88–92)

Even earlier, Talbot had rallied his English forces against the French "curs" by calling them "timorous deer" who ought to transform themselves into "desperate stags" and "turn on the bloody hounds with heads of steel" (*1 Henry VI* 4.2.45–52). But by the time of *Julius Caesar,* such Ovidian metamorphosing of violence was a thing of the past, an idiom Shakespeare had experimented with, found wanting, and discarded. Antony, in reverting to it, deliberately sets Caesar's murder in an outmoded context: the language is showy enough to persuade the conspirators that he is a man of noble feeling but artificial enough to indicate that Antony is speaking from the mind, not from the heart.

The dispassionate ease with which Antony adopts expedient voices allows him inevitably to get the better of Brutus. Brutus tries manfully to identify himself by the heroic forms he enacts; he denies that there is any disparity between idiom and selfhood. Antony admits the disparity and thus is free to play on it as he sees fit. The divorce between acting and being causes no dilemma in Antony as it does in Brutus. A particular idiom does not define his character; the self-consciousness to play roles defined by the idiom does. Lest I be thought to mean that Antony is no more than an impostor, however, let me issue a caveat. The audience's awareness that Antony has a selfhood deeper than his idiom dawns only gradually. When he laments over Caesar, offers his breast to the conspirators' swords, shakes their hands, mourns the hunting of a noble hart, and swears to avenge the murder and appease Caesar's ghost, the audience may believe in the rhetorical reality of his character. Only in retrospect— and the moment of discovery will differ for each of us—will the audience appreciate that rhetoric and character are distinct from one another. Antony's idiom shifts, not for the reason York's shifts between the second and third parts of *Henry VI*—that is, to satisfy Shakespeare's rhetorical design, but because by those shifts, Shakespeare can dramatize in Antony a dynamic process of thought that psychologically justifies the choice of idiom. Motivated by political self-interest, Antony himself has both the reason and the autonomy, lacking in Shakespeare's early heroes, to manipulate rhetorical conventions: Shakespeare allows him to usurp his own prerogative to determine character by rhetorical means. As one moves chronologically through the scene of Caesar's death, therefore, Shakespeare preserves conventional modes of speech as momentarily adequate to define traditional attitudes and types of heroism, as if he, in a manner of old, has applied character with rhetorical brushstrokes; but in a retrospective analysis of all such moments, we realize that he has been forging new criteria for determining heroic character. Antony *is* the roles he plays in sequence, but the reality of his character is more than the sum of his parts.

As with Antony, so with the play. In a sense, Shakespeare satisfies conventional expectations of blood tragedy in the cosmic unrest, the ritual slaughter, the scenes of civil discord, the appearance of the ghost. He also satisfies expectations of heroic tragedy in Caesar's de casibus fall, the noble reconciliation of Brutus and Cassius, the stoicism of Brutus's suicide, even in the conventional elegies spoken over Cassius—"The sun of Rome is set. Our day is gone" (5.3.63)—and over Brutus—"This was the noblest Roman of them all" (5.5.68). But he does so only after exposing the conventions of heroism to ironic scrutiny, occasionally (as in Caesar's bombast) to parody, and finding them inadequate to represent a heroic reality. Heroism in *Julius Caesar* becomes real when Shakespeare holds conventions at arm's length—cuts traditional heroic patterns out of well-worn cloth only so that characters, scenes, the play itself, may try them on and complain, "These don't fit. They're yesterday's fashion. Fustian! We have outgrown them."

Chronology

1564	William Shakespeare born at Stratford-on-Avon to John Shakespeare, a butcher, and Mary Arden. He is baptized on April 26.
1582	Marries Anne Hathaway in November.
1583	Daughter Susanna born, baptized on May 26.
1585	Twins Hamnet and Judith born, baptized on February 2.
1588–90	Sometime during these years, Shakespeare goes to London, without family. First plays performed in London.
1590–92	*The Comedy of Errors,* the three parts of *Henry VI.*
1593–94	Publication of *Venus and Adonis* and *The Rape of Lucrece,* both dedicated to the Earl of Southampton. Shakespeare becomes a sharer in the Lord Chamberlain's company of actors. *The Taming of the Shrew, The Two Gentlemen of Verona, Richard III, Titus Andronicus.*
1595–97	*Romeo and Juliet, Richard II, King John, A Midsummer Night's Dream, Love's Labor's Lost.*
1596	Son Hamnet dies. Grant of arms to Shakespeare's father.
1597	*The Merchant of Venice, Henry IV, Part 1.* Purchases New Place in Stratford.
1598–1600	*Henry IV, Part 2, As You Like It, Much Ado about Nothing, Twelfth Night, The Merry Wives of Windsor, Henry V* and *Julius Caesar.* Moves his company to the new Globe Theatre.
1601	*Hamlet.* Shakespeare's father dies, buried on September 8.
1601–2	*Troilus and Cressida.*

1603	Death of Queen Elizabeth; James VI of Scotland becomes James I of England; Shakespeare's company becomes the King's Men.
1603–4	*All's Well That Ends Well, Measure for Measure, Othello.*
1605–6	*King Lear, Macbeth.*
1607	Marriage of daughter Susanna on June 5.
1607–8	*Timon of Athens, Antony and Cleopatra, Pericles, Coriolanus.*
1608	Shakespeare's mother dies, buried on September 9.
1609	*Cymbeline,* publication of sonnets. Shakespeare's company purchases Blackfriars Theatre.
1610–11	*The Winter's Tale, The Tempest.* Shakespeare retires to Stratford.
1612–13	*Henry VIII, The Two Noble Kinsmen.*
1616	Marriage of daughter Judith on February 10. Shakespeare dies at Stratford on April 23.
1623	Publication of the Folio edition of Shakespeare's plays.

Contributors

HAROLD BLOOM, Sterling Professor of the Humanities at Yale University, is the author of *The Anxiety of Influence, Poetry and Repression,* and many other volumes of literary criticism. His forthcoming study, *Freud: Transference and Authority*, attempts a full-scale reading of all of Freud's major writings. A MacArthur Prize Fellow, he is general editor of five series of literary criticism published by Chelsea House. During 1987–88, he served as Charles Eliot Norton Professor of Poetry at Harvard University.

DEREK TRAVERSI is the author of *An Approach to Shakespeare, The Canterbury Tales: A Reading,* and *T. S. Eliot: The Longer Poems.*

LAWRENCE DANSON, Professor of English at Princeton University, is the author of *The Harmonies of the Merchant of Venice* and the editor of *On King Lear.*

MARJORIE B. GARBER, Professor of English at Harvard University, is the author of many articles on Shakespeare, Marlowe, and Milton. She is also the author of *Dream in Shakespeare: From Metaphor to Metamorphosis* and *Coming of Age in Shakespeare*, a study of maturation patterns and rites of passage in the plays.

MICHAEL LONG, Professor of English at the University of Hawaii at Manoa, is the author of *Marvell and Nabokov: Childhood and Arcadia.*

NAOMI CONN LIEBLER is Assistant Professor of English at Montclair State College, New Jersey.

Anne Barton is Fellow of New College and University Lecturer in English at Oxford. She is author of *Shakespeare and the Idea of the Play* and *Ben Jonson, Dramatist,* and is one of the editors of the *Riverside Shakespeare.*

Jonathan Goldberg is Professor of English at Johns Hopkins University and the author of *Endless Worke: Spenser and the Structure of Discourse* and *Voice Terminal Echo: A Study of* The Tempest *and the Logic of Allegorical Expression.*

A. D. Nuttall is Professor of English at the University of Sussex and the author of *A Common Sky,* Crime and Punishment: *Murder as a Philosophic Experiment,* and *A New Mimesis.*

James C. Bulman is Professor of English at Allegheny College and the author of *Comedy from Shakespeare to Sheridan.*

Bibliography

Anderson, Peter S. "Shakespeare's *Caesar*: The Language of Sacrifice." *Comparative Drama* 3 (1969): 3–26.

Arthos, John. "The Waste of Man." In *Shakespeare's Use of Dream and Vision,* 111–35. London: Bowes & Bowes, 1977.

Bellringer, A. W. "*Julius Caesar.*" In *Room Enough in Shakespeare's Wide and Universal Stage,* edited by C. B. Cox and D. J. Palmer, 146–63. Manchester: Manchester University Press, 1984.

Bligh, John. "Cicero's Choric Comment in *Julius Caesar.*" *English Studies in Canada* 8 (1982): 391–408.

Brooke, Nicholas. *Shakespeare's Early Tragedies.* London: Methuen, 1968.

Burckhardt, Sigurd. *Shakespearean Meanings.* Princeton: Princeton University Press, 1968.

Charlton, H. B. *Shakespearean Tragedy,* 69–82. Cambridge: Cambridge University Press, 1949.

Charney, Maurice. *Shakespeare's Roman Plays: The Function of Imagery in the Drama.* Cambridge: Harvard University Press, 1961.

Colie, Rosalie L. *Shakespeare's Living Art.* Princeton: Princeton University Press, 1974.

Dean, Leonard F., ed. *Twentieth Century Interpretations of* Julius Caesar. Englewood Cliffs, N.J.: Prentice-Hall, 1968.

Dorsch, T. S. Introduction to *The Arden Shakespeare: Julius Caesar.* London: Methuen, 1955.

Durham, Mildred. "Drama of the Dying God in *Julius Caesar.*" *Hartford Studies in Literature* 11 (1979): 49–57.

Ebel, Henry. "Caesar's Wounds: A Study of William Shakespeare." *Psychoanalytic Review* 62 (1975): 107–30.

Evans, Bertrand. "The Blind and the Blinded." In *Shakespeare's Tragic Practice,* 52–74. Oxford: Oxford University Press, 1979.

Evans, Gareth Lloyd. *The Upstart Crow.* London: J. M. Dent, 1982.

Gerenday, Lynn de. "Play, Ritualization, and Ambivalence in *Julius Caesar.*" *Literature and Psychology* 24 (1974): 24–33.

Granville-Barker, Harley. *Prefaces to Shakespeare.* Princeton: Princeton University Press, 1975.

Hartsock, Mildred E. "The Complexity of *Julius Caesar.*" *PMLA* 81 (1966): 56–62.

Herbert, Edward T. "Myth and Archetype in *Julius Caesar*." *Literature and Psychology* 57 (1970): 303–8.

Jorgensen,Paul A. *William Shakespeare: The Tragedies*. Boston: Twayne, 1985.

Knight, G. Wilson. "The Eroticism of *Julius Caesar*." In *The Imperial Theme,* 63–95. Oxford: Oxford University Press, 1931.

MacCallum, M. W. *Shakespeare's Roman Plays and Their Background*. 1910. Reprint. New York: Russell & Russell, 1967.

McAlindon, Thomas. "The Numbering of Men and Days: Symbolic Design in the Tragedy of *Julius Caesar*." *Studies in Philology* 81 (1984): 372–93.

Mack, Maynard. "*Julius Caesar*." In *Modern Shakespearean Criticism*, edited by Alvin B. Kernan, 290–300. New York: Harcourt, Brace, 1970.

Miller, Antony. "The Roman State in *Julius Caesar* and *Sejanus*." In *Jonson and Shakespeare*, edited by Ian Donaldson, 179–201. London: Macmillan, 1983.

Palmer, John. *Political Characters of Shakespeare*. London: Macmillan, 1957.

Pechter, Edward. "*Julius Caesar* and *Sejanus*: Roman Politics, Inner Selves, and the Powers of the Theatre." In *Shakespeare and His Contemporaries*, edited by E. A. J. Honigmann, 60–78. Manchester: Manchester University Press, 1986.

Prosner, Matthew N. *The Heroic Image in Five Shakespearean Tragedies*. Princeton: Princeton University Press, 1965.

Rabkin, Norman. *Shakespeare and the Common Understanding*. New York: Free Press, 1968.

———. *Shakespeare and the Problem of Meaning*. Chicago: University of Chicago Press, 1981.

Ribner, Irving. *Patterns in Shakespearean Tragedy*. London: Methuen, 1960.

Ridley, M. R. *Shakespeare's Plays*. London: J. M. Dent, 1957.

Schanzer, Ernest. *The Problem Plays of Shakespeare*. New York: Schocken, 1963.

Simmons, J. L. *Shakespeare's Pagan World*. Charlottesville: University Press of Virginia, 1973.

Smith, Warren D. "The Duplicate Revelation of Portia's Death." *Shakespeare Quarterly* 4 (1953): 153–61.

Stirling, Brents. "Brutus and the Death of Portia." *Shakespeare Quarterly* 10 (1959): 211–18.

———. "*Julius Caesar* in Revision." *Shakespeare Quarterly* 13 (1962): 187–206.

———. *Unity in Shakespearean Tragedy*. New York: Columbia University Press, 1956.

Ure, Peter, ed. *Shakespeare:* Julius Caesar Casebook Series. London: Methuen, 1969.

Van Laan, Thomas F. *Role Playing in Shakespeare*. Toronto: Toronto University Press, 1978.

Velz, John W. "Orator and Imperator in *Julius Caesar*: Style and the Process of Roman History." *Shakespeare Studies* 15 (1982): 55–76.

Whitaker, Virgil K. *The Mirror Up to Nature*. San Marino, Calif.: The Huntington Library, 1965.

Wilson, H. S. *On the Design of Shakespearean Tragedy*. Toronto: Toronto University Press, 1957.

Zeeveld, W. Gordon. *The Temper of Shakespeare's Thought*. New Haven: Yale University Press, 1974.

Acknowledgments

"*Julius Caesar:* The Roman Tragedy" (originally entitled "*Julius Caesar*") by Derek Traversi from *An Approach to Shakespeare 2:* Troilus and Cressida *to* The Tempest, 3d ed., by Derek Traversi, © 1969 by Derek Traversi. Reprinted by permission of Hollis and Carter.

"Ritual and *Julius Caesar*" (originally entitled "*Julius Caesar*") by Lawrence Danson from *Tragic Alphabet: Shakespeare's Drama of Language* by Lawrence Danson, © 1974 by Yale University. Reprinted by permission of Yale University Press.

"Dream and Interpretation: *Julius Caesar*" by Marjorie B. Garber from *Dream in Shakespeare: From Metaphor to Metamorphosis* by Marjorie B. Garber, © 1974 by Yale University. Reprinted by permission of Yale University Press.

"*Julius Caesar:* Social Order and the Kinetic World" (originally entitled "The Civility of Marcus Brutus") by Michael Long from *The Unnatural Scene* by Michael Long, © 1976 by Michael Long. Reprinted by permission of Methuen & Co.

" 'Thou Bleeding Piece of Earth': The Ritual Ground of *Julius Caesar*" by Naomi Conn Liebler from *Shakespeare Studies* 14 (1981), © 1981 by the Council for Research in the Renaissance. Reprinted by permission.

"Rhetoric in Ancient Rome" (originally entitled "Julius Caesar and Coriolanus: Shakespeare's Roman World of Words") by Anne Barton from *Shakespeare's Craft: Eight Lectures,* edited by Philip H. Highfill, Jr., © 1982 by The George Washington University. Reprinted by permission of the author and The George Washington University.

"The Roman Actor: *Julius Caesar*" (originally entitled "The Roman Actor: *Julius Caesar, Sejanus, Coriolanus, Catiline,* and *The Roman Actor")* by Jonathan Goldberg from *James I and the Politics of Literature: Jonson, Shakespeare, Donne, and Their Contemporaries* by Jonathan Goldberg, © 1983 by The Johns Hopkins University Press, Baltimore/London. Reprinted by permission of The Johns Hopkins University Press.

139

"Brutus's Nature and Shakespeare's Art" (originally entitled "*Julius Caesar* and *Coriolanus:* How Roman are the Roman Plays of Shakespeare?") by A. D. Nuttall from *A New Mimesis* by A. D. Nuttall, © 1983 by A. D. Nuttall. Reprinted by permission of Methuen & Co.

"Ironic Heroism in *Julius Caesar:* A Repudiation of the Past" (originally entitled "Ironic Heroism: A Repudiation of the Past") by James C. Bulman from *The Heroic Idiom of Shakespearean Tragedy* by James C. Bulman, © 1985 by Associated University Presses, Inc. Reprinted by permission of Associated University Presses, Inc.

Index

Aeneid (Virgil), 2, 109, 116
Andronicus, Titus (*Titus Andronicus*), 123, 130
Antony, 6, 9, 39, 46, 87, 101, 131; as absolutist, 93; and Brutus, 2, 17, 55, 58, 61, 95, 129; and Caesar, 31, 33, 69, 80, 95, 102–4; and Cassius, 11; coldness of, 74–75; and death of Brutus, 3, 26–27, 41, 59, 132; funeral oration of, 18, 35–36, 37, 72, 74, 85, 117, 129–30; and history, 73; and Iago, 116; as Lupercus, 70; moral limitations of, 17–18, 19; and revenge idiom, 126–31; and sacrifice image, 39, 70–71, 72
Antony and Cleopatra, 5, 40–41, 53, 84, 93, 106
Appian, 62
Aristotle, 80–81, 110
As You Like It, 2
Aufidius (*Coriolanus*), 33, 89, 128
Augustine, St., 109

Bacon, Francis, 82
Baker, Margaret, 77
Banquo's ghost (*Macbeth*), 45
Batman, Stephan, 63
Bonjour, Adrien, 39
Brutus, 1, 9–10, 31, 39, 84, 112; as actor, 94; and Antony, 2, 17–18, 55, 58, 61, 95, 129; Antony's elegy for, 3, 26–27, 41, 59, 89, 132; as author of tragedy, 33–36, 37, 125–26; and

Caesar, 7, 20, 33, 51, 72–73, 123; and Cassius, 20–25, 94–97; and Cicero, 80; and confusion of symbol, 31–32, 34–35, 38; as conservative, 74, 117, 118; contradictory character of, 12–16, 26; dishonesty of, 86, 87–88, 123–25; and emotions, 16; errors of, 72–73, 85; and friendship, 12–13; guilt of, 45; and heroic idiom, 124–26, 131; and history, 73, 74; honor of, 11–12, 21, 98–99; idealism of, 13, 15, 64, 67, 69–70, 123–24; influence of Cassius on, 10–12, 14, 47, 87, 112; and language, 30; and love, 96–97; and Marullus, 68; moral spontaneity of, 2, 118; naming of, 87, 89, 99; nobility of, 25–26; and personal vs. public, 6, 96–100; and Portia, 9, 24, 65, 118; reasoning of, 113–16; self-praise of, 3–4, 11; sterility of, 55–58, 60; suicide of, 14, 19, 131; and theater, 91, 92, 94, 100; as tragic hero, 32, 36, 40–41, 53–60; unawareness of, 32, 44–45; as virtuous, 54–55. *See also* Stoicism
Brutus (*Caesar's Revenge*), 125

Caesar, 6–7, 8, 33, 65–66, 72–73, 96; absence of, 95–96; as actor, 92, 100–101; blindness of, 48–49, 51; and Calpurnia's dream, 48–50; death of, 16, 69, 125–26; and false

Caesar (continued)
sacrifice, 39; as friend, 12–13; ghost of, 45, 88; hubris of, 46, 122, 123; inconsistency of, 7–9; mantle of, 102–4; and misinterpretation, 47; offer of crown to, 31, 80, 94; personal vs. public in character of, 52; and poets, 38; and rhetoric, 84; self-naming of, 7, 86–87; superstitiousness of, 30, 44, 46, 61; as tragic hero, 32, 33–36; weakness of, 1, 65, 86, 96, 99, 122–23
Caesar's Revenge, 121, 125, 127
Calpurnia, 3, 7, 8, 61, 123; sterility of, 30, 46, 61, 65, 96
Calpurnia's dream, 9, 43, 44, 68, 84, 100; importance of, 47–51; in Plutarch, 50–51, 69
Carlisle (Richard II), 128
Casca, 31, 65; and Caesar, 7, 33, 101; and omens, 46–47, 48, 68–69, 79–80, 100
Cassius, 2, 11, 34, 39–40, 68, 102; and anger, 57; and Antony, 11, 14, 129; and Brutus, 20–25, 55–56; and Caesar, 7, 20, 33, 86, 100–101, 123; and Cicero, 14, 80; and dreams, 44; elegies for, 132; and history, 73, 74; and honor, 99, 102; influence on Brutus of, 10–12, 14, 47, 87, 112; insight of, 32; and irony, 35; and language, 30; nominalism of, 37; and omens, 69, 79–80; and personal vs. public, 96–100; and Portia's death, 24, 118, 119, 120; suicide of, 25, 43; and theater, 94
Cassius (Caesar's Revenge), 125
Catiline (Jonson), 82–83
Cato, 73
Chamberlain, John, 92
Charney, Maurice, 77
Cicero, 14, 31, 68, 74–75, 79–82, 111; and omens, 46–47, 79
Cicero (Catiline), 82–83
Cinna, 16, 51
Cinna the poet, 19, 37–38, 39, 43, 51–52
City of God (Augustine), 109
Clarence (Henry VI), 125
Clarence (Richard III), 44
Claudius, 45
Cleopatra (Antony and Cleopatra), 40–41, 93

Clifford (Henry VI), 124, 127
Conspirators: as actors, 91–92; and Brutus, 14, 15–16; cold-bloodedness of, 51; hysterical language of, 9; inconsistency of, 17
Cooper, 62–63
Coriolanus, 5, 33, 53, 88, 124, 128; anachronism in, 106; rhetoric in, 83, 85, 89

Dante, 89
Decius Brutus, 8, 9, 34, 84, 129; and Calpurnia's dream, 44, 47, 49–50, 51
Dictionary (Elyot), 63
Dido (Aeneid), 109, 116
Die Charakterprobleme bei Shakespeare (Schucking), 105
Dodds, E. R., 111

Edmund (King Lear), 37
Edward (Henry VI), 125
Edward (Richard III), 44
Epicureanism, 108, 110
Epicurus, 108
Explorations (Knights), 106

Falstaff (1 & 2 Henry IV), 2, 106
Fasti (Ovid), 62, 63
Feast of the Lupercal, 61–78
Flavius, 29, 31, 85
Frost, Robert, 41

Gloucester (Richard III), 44, 45
Golden Book of the Leaden Gods (Batman), 63
Gorboduc (Sackville and Norton), 127
Gorgias (Plato), 80
Granville-Barker, Harley, 39
Greeks and the Irrational, The (Dodds), 111

Hamlet (Hamlet), 29, 41, 94, 113–14, 116, 129; and Brutus, 1, 10, 31, 32
Hamlet, 2, 33, 48, 113–14, 116, 129; blocking of expression in, 31, 32; language in, 29, 30; theater in, 94
Hassel, R. Chris, Jr., 78
Hastings (Richard III), 44

Henry IV (*Henry IV*), 45
Henry IV, 2, 5, 11, 45
Henry V (*Henry V*), 127
Henry V, 2, 5, 127
Henry VI, 124, 125, 126, 127, 128, 130
Hermione (*The Winter's Tale*), 49
Heywood, Thomas, 94
Hieronimo (*Spanish Tragedie*), 128
Holofernes (*Love's Labor's Lost*), 57
Homer, 111
Horatio (*Spanish Tragedie*), 128
Hotspur (*Henry IV*), 11–12

Iago (*Othello*), 115, 116
Iliad (Homer), 111

James I, 92–93, 96, 99
Jocasta, 127
Johnson, Samuel, 3
Jonson, Ben, 82–83

King Lear, 5, 37, 41
Knights, L. C., 106
Kyd, Thomas, 122, 128

Laertes (*Hamlet*), 33
Lavinia (*Titus Andronicus*), 130
Leishman, J. B., 108
Lepidus, 19, 74–75
Lewis, C. S., 107
Life and Reign of James I (Wilson), 91
Ligarius, 65
Lives of the Noble Grecians and Romans
    (Plutarch), 1, 5, 52, 81, 88–89, 108;
    Brutus in, 57, 59–60, 72; Caesar in,
    69–70, 72–73; Caesar's ghost in, 45;
    Calpurnia's dream in, 50–51, 69;
    Feast of the Lupercal in, 62, 63–67;
    omens in, 46; ritual in, 77
Livy, 62
Locrine, 122
Love's Labor's Lost, 57
Lucilius, 20, 41
Lucius, 45
Lucretius, 110
Lupercalia. *See* Feast of the Lupercal

Macbeth (*Macbeth*), 45, 58
Macbeth, 5, 17, 36, 45, 58

Marcus (*Titus Andronicus*), 130
Margaret (*Henry VI*), 128
Marlowe, Christopher, 122, 127
Measure for Measure, 53–54
Menenius, 85
The Merchant of Venice, 76
Mercutio (*Romeo and Juliet*), 60
Messala, 26, 88–89, 118
Metamorphoses (Ovid), 62
Metellus, 129
A Midsummer Night's Dream, 56
Milton, John, 59
Montaigne, Michel de, 81, 82, 84
Murellus, 29, 31, 65, 68, 69

Nietzsche, Freidrich, 53, 55, 57
North, Thomas, 5, 6, 60, 63
Norton, Thomas, 127
Nuttall, A. D., 2

Octavius, 20, 25, 26, 27, 44, 88; cold-
    ness of, 19, 74–75; and death of
    Brutus, 59; and hunting image, 39;
    as unpersuadable, 84–85
Octavius (*Antony and Cleopatra*), 41
Of the Colours of Good and Evil (Bacon), 82
"On the Vanitie of Words" (Mon-
    taigne), 81
Orsino (*Twelfth Night*), 130
Othello, 87, 115, 116
Ovid, 62, 63, 130

Plato, 80, 81, 110, 118
Plutarch. *See Lives of the Noble Grecians*
    and Romans
Polonius (*Hamlet*), 94
Pompey, 74, 85
Pope, Alexander, 108
Popper, Sir Karl, 118
Portia, 24, 68, 73, 97, 118; and Brutus,
    9, 65
Publius, 19

Rabkin, Norman, 74
Rhetoric, 80–89
Rhetoric (Aristotle), 81
Richard (*Henry VI*), 125
Richard II, 128

Richard III (*Richard III*), 45
Richard III, 44, 45
Roman populace: and Caesar's death, 68; language of, 29; as mob, 18, 19; passivity of, 85; and ritual, 29–30
Romeo (*Romeo and Juliet*), 49, 50
Romeo and Juliet, 49, 50, 60
Romulus (*Life of Romulus*), 64–67
Rosalind (*As You Like It*), 2
Rumelin, Gustav, 105
Rutland (*Henry VI*), 128

Sackville, Thomas, 127
Schopenhauer, Arthur, 53, 55, 60
Schucking, Levin, 105
Scott, Sir Walter, 108
Sejanus (Jonson), 83
Seneca, 1, 82, 108, 110–11, 121, 127
Shakespeare and the Common Understanding (Rabkin), 74
Shakespeare's plays: audiences of, 75; criticism of, 32–33, 105–6; dreams in, 49; ghosts in, 45–46; hero in, 121; historical basis of, 5–6, 106–7; history in, 75; politics in, 1, 4, 12; revenge idiom in, 127–28; ritual in, 76; Stoicism in, 111–12; style in, 6; tragic moment in, 36; unchanging society in, 59
Shakespearestudien (Rumelin), 105
Socrates, 110
Socrates (*Gorgias*), 80
Soothsayer, 30, 46
Spanish Tragedie (Kyd), 122, 128
Spencer, T. J. B., 75
Stephanus, Charles, 63
Stirling, Brents, 119, 120
Stoicism, 3, 108–11; and emotional control, 24–25, 58–59, 116, 118, 119, 120; and inwardness, 10, 112; and morality, 1–2, 55, 60; and tragic hero, 36
Stoll, E. E., 105
Strato, 26, 41, 89
Structure of Julius Caesar, The (Bonjour), 39

Tacitus, 82
Talbot (*Henry VI*), 127, 130
Tamburlaine the Great (Marlowe), 122, 127
Thesaurus (Stephanus), 63
Thesaurus Linguae Romanae & Britannicae (Cooper), 62–63

Theseus (*A Midsummer Night's Dream*), 56
Tiberius, 92
Titinius, 25, 47, 68, 118; suicide of, 39, 40, 43
Titus Andronicus, 123, 124, 125, 130
Tragedy of Julius Caesar, The: ambiguity in, 68–69; anachronism in, 106; audiences of, 75–76, 78; blood in, 17, 78, 88; cataclysm in, 67, 69, 80, 128; as centered on single event, 6–7; confusion of symbol in, 29–31, 37–40, 63; contradictions in, 12, 13, 26; criticism of, 32–33, 61; cynicism in, 18–19; death in, 18; disease images in, 65, 69; dramatic presentations of, 1; emotions in, 16–17; fatalism in, 8; Feast of the Lupercal in, 61–68, 70, 76–78; heroic conventions in, 32–36, 121–32; historical basis of, 5–6, 41, 67, 75–76, 78, 108; history in, 73–74; image of mirror in, 11, 112; irony in, 2, 3, 35, 38, 50, 54, 59; language in, 7, 29, 30; limitations of, 3, 14, 53–54; love in, 96–97; misinterpretation in, 43–52; offstage scenes in, 94–95, 96; personal vs. public in, 5, 6, 52, 96–100, 124; poets in, 38, 56–57; politics of, 1, 33; portrayal of Roman culture in, 108, 117–18; rhetoric in, 84–89; ritual in, 72, 76–77; sacrifice image in, 38–40, 69–72; Stoicism in, 1–2, 25; structure of, 33; text of, 119, 120; theater in, 91–104, 125–26
Translating Horace (Leishman), 108–9
Troilus and Cressida, 25, 53, 97, 128
Twelfth Night, 130

Ulysses (*Troilus and Cressida*), 128

Varro, 45
Virgil, 2, 108, 109, 116
Volumnia (*Coriolanus*), 124

Warwick (*Henry VI*), 126
Wilson, Arthur, 91
Winter's Tale, The, 49

York (*Henry VI*), 124, 128

Zeno, 108